The Nonfiction Book Marketing and Launch Plan:

Build Your Audience and Sell More Books

A Workbook and Planning Guide

Stephanie Chandler

THE NONFICTION BOOK MARKETING AND LAUNCH PLAN
Build Your Audience and Sell More Books
A Workbook and Planning Guide
by Stephanie Chandler

1. LAN027000 2. LAN002000 3. BUS043000
ISBN: 978-1-949642-85-8 (Spiral Binding)
ISBN: 978-1-949642-86-5 (Paperback)
ISBN: 978-1-949642-87-2 (Ebook)

Cover design by Lewis Agrell

Printed in the United States of America

Authority Publishing
13389 Folsom Blvd. Ste. 300-256
Folsom, CA 95630
AuthorityPublishing.com

Table of Contents

PART I

Set the Foundation

CHAPTER I

Become an Influencer in Your Field

As an author in the world of nonfiction, book sales may be a top goal, though perhaps not your only goal. Many of us who write nonfiction do so because we want to make a difference in the world. That might mean sharing your personal journey in hopes of enlightening others on a similar path, teaching readers a new skill, or introducing readers to a fresh concept or insight. Many of us want to make a dent in the universe, and writing books gives us an opportunity to do so.

Your book might also be used as a business card to attract speaking engagements, consulting clients, or other new business opportunities. And if your book is a tool for business purposes, the number of books you sell may not matter as much as the *number of new opportunities you can generate because of your book*.

Whatever your motivation for writing and publishing your book, as an author it is likely your primary goal is to reach more people. Unfortunately, most authors do this the hard way. I started out that way too.

Several years ago, I was part of a big book launch for one of the *Chicken Soup for the Soul* books. It was held in Sacramento, and we received a ton of media coverage on the morning of the event. The local morning news show and several radio stations interviewed us and promoted the event to our community.

We arrived at Barnes and Noble just before they opened and were excited to find our table just steps inside the front door. It was prime real estate, and we were ready for the big day!

One of the book contributors was Shari Fitzpatrick, founder of Shari's Berries. She brought delicious chocolate-covered strawberries for visitors to enjoy.

While the picture you see here looks like we are busy, the reality is we weren't busy at all—at least not after all the free chocolate-covered berries were gone. The shopper on the right is a friend of one of the contributors, and the shopper on the left is my mom.

Despite all the phenomenal media coverage we received, the berries were the biggest hit of the day, not the books. Shoppers greeted us and thanked us for their treats, but the vast majority left without purchasing a single copy. After three hours sitting in front of the entrance, guess how many copies we sold? A grand total of eight books.

That was the day I swore I would never do another book-signing event.

Know How Many Books You Want to Sell

Book-signing events at bookstores are a popular way many authors seek to sell books. And while you can certainly schedule events at retailers across the country, there is a harsh reality you will likely face along the way: most book-signing events for unknown authors generate just a handful of book sales. They also require a lot of time and effort. (As a former bookstore owner and fellow writer, I speak from experience.)

Unless you promote your book-signing event and drive people through the doors, you will likely discover that these events can be a frustrating waste of time. In fact, there is a good chance you will spend more time directing customers to the bathroom than actually making sales. (Sad, but true!)

While it may sound fun and glamourous to sit in a bookstore autographing books, these events rarely live up to expectations. More importantly, a book-signing event focuses on selling just one copy of your book at a time, requiring too much time and effort to generate each sale.

Would you rather sell a single copy or many copies at a time?

There are three primary ways to sell large quantities of books:

1. Sell bulk quantities of books to buyers directly.
2. Invest in paid advertising.
3. *Build a loyal audience of fans who eagerly buy your books and tell others to do the same.* (Winner, winner, chicken dinner!)

The primary focus of this workbook is on building a loyal audience because this is the secret sauce to creating long-term success as an author. However, paid advertising and bulk sales are covered in chapter 19 so keep reading.

Get Ready to Work (Book Marketing Is Not for Sissies)

As you may have discovered by now, book marketing is not an easy job. If you have been an author for a while, you've probably tried various methods and have been frustrated or disappointed with many of them. You are not alone. For most new authors, and even for those of us who have been at it for years, book sales results can be disappointing.

Part of the challenge is that most people don't read books. According to a study by Pew Research, the average American reads twelve books per year. And that number represents a mix of avid readers and people who read little or not at all. The data suggests that the median number of books read in a year is actually just four titles. FOUR BOOKS! Sadly, twenty-seven percent of respondents admitted to not reading a single book in the prior year. Yikes. (And yet we watch countless hours of crime shows on Netflix each week. Spread the word—books are cool!)

So, if the average person is reading just four books per year, we must work extra hard to earn each and every reader's purchase. It is our job to convince readers that our books are well worth their limited reading time.

To further complicate matters, most people choose books based on reviews and recommendations. When a friend, journalist, or someone we respect recommends a book, we are far more likely to buy. This same rule applies to recommendations for movies, TV shows, and restaurants.

I was reminded how powerful recommendations can be after chatting with a friend and mentioning how much I enjoyed *10% Happier: How I Tamed the Voice in My Head, Reduced Stress Without Losing My Edge, and Found Self-Help That Actually Works—A True Story* by Dan Harris. I suggested she'd like it too. Fast-forward a week later. She went on vacation and snapped a picture of herself reading the book, then posted it to her personal profile on Facebook. That photo generated dozens of comments from her friends, many of whom reported they also enjoyed the book, or thanking her for the recommendation because her post prompted them to want to read it too.

Readers also buy products and services based on reviews and recommendations from media outlets. When *People* magazine reviews a book, the sales for the book instantly get a major boost, often toward *New York Times* Best Sellers status. (Which, by the way, is vastly different from "best seller" status on Amazon. We'll talk about this more in chapter 14.) When a blogger recommends a book to her loyal audience of readers, book sales follow. When a popular podcaster, YouTuber, or social media influencer raves about a book, people listen.

When it comes to influencers and marketing, you have two choices. You can connect with influencers in your field and contribute to their podcasts, blogs, and other programs. Or you can build your own audience and become an influencer yourself. (And better yet, do both.)

Become an Influencer in Your Field

An influencer is an author, blogger, speaker, social media star, celebrity, podcaster, TV show host, or anyone with a substantial number of loyal fans. CBS reported that Kylie Jenner earns $1 million for a single post to the more than 130 million followers on her Instagram account. Soccer star Cristiano Ronaldo commands $750,000 per sponsored post. Popular YouTube gamer PewDiePie earns upwards of $12 million per year in ad revenue, based on the astonishing numbers of views his videos receive. (For some inexplicable reason, kids enjoy watching people play video games.)

Results like these extend to bloggers and other people authors can relate to:

- Kayla Itsines is an Australian fitness blogger who sells downloadable e-books from her website and has more than ten million social media followers.
- Rachel Brathen is known as @yoga_girl to her two million Instagram followers, and her *Yoga Girl* book has hundreds of positive reviews on Amazon.
- Tyler Oakley is a LGBTQ activist and author, and a highly paid social media influencer with more than seven million YouTube subscribers. According to Izea.com, he earns more than $6 million per year.
- Lilly Singh is a comedian with more than fourteen million followers on YouTube, five million on X (formerly known as Twitter), and three million on Facebook. It should be no surprise that her first book, *How to Be a Bawse: A Guide to Conquering Life*, hit the *New York Times* Best Sellers list following its release in 2017.
- Clea Shearer and Joanna Templin are the founders of The Home Edit, a professional organizing service. They are authors of two books about home organization and have nearly four million followers on Instagram, which led them to land their own TV series on Netflix.
- Brené Brown got her big break after receiving an invitation to speak at TEDxHouston. After the video was promoted to the main TED.com home page, it went viral and her whole life changed. She's since authored several *New York Times* Best Sellers, *been featured on Oprah* and countless media outlets, and has produced several Netflix specials.

Curious how influencer earnings are calculated? According to Digiday.com, influencers earn an average of $1,000 per one hundred thousand followers on Instagram, while YouTubers earn around $2,000 per one hundred thousand followers.

Own Your Niche and Your Influence

The following authors have carved out a seat at the influencer table within their respective niche communities. These are regular people just like you and me who started from square one and put in the work to market their books.

- Dr. Saundra Dalton-Smith is a physician and author of several books. In support of her book *Sacred Rest: Recover Your Life, Renew Your Energy, Restore Your Sanity*, she participated in dozens of media interviews. Any author who has done a media tour, including yours truly, can tell you that media exposure doesn't always lead to book sales. So, Dr. Dalton-Smith decided to create a quiz using a free WordPress plugin. (You can take it at RestQuiz.com.) When I asked how many have taken her quiz, she reported more than two hundred thousand people. Considering each person had to share an email address to take the quiz, she clearly created a phenomenal tool to build her tribe!
- Karl Palachuk is a dear friend of mine, and together we coauthored *The Nonfiction Book Publishing Plan*. Karl teaches owners of IT companies how to build their technology businesses. This is a teeny, tiny niche, but it's been netting big revenues for Karl for years. He earns a comfortable living from book sales, speaking engagements, corporate sponsorships, and consulting. He also hosts an online store where he sells *five figures per month* in recordings, templates, worksheets, and other digital downloads.
- Melinda Emerson is a small-business consultant who decided to start a weekly interview series on X (formerly known as Twitter) called #SmallBizChat. She branded herself as The Small Biz Lady and invited guests to join her each week. This effort generated a following of more than three hundred thousand followers on the platform, and it led to a book deal with a traditional press plus hundreds of speaking engagements and corporate sponsorship relationships. She was also invited to develop a series of online courses in partnership with Drexel University.

As you can see from these examples, you don't need millions of followers to position yourself as an influencer in your field. You need to cultivate a tribe of loyal fans, and that's much easier to do when you carve out a niche.

I also want to make it clear; social media is not the end-all, be-all. It is one of many tools available for authors. But it's essential to understand that to become an influencer, you must have a following of fans somewhere. That could be on a social media site, your email list, or through a national column that you write.

Use Influencer Marketing to Create Revenue Opportunities

One of the most buzzed-about terms in PR and marketing is "influencer marketing." The term is making its way into job descriptions and titles of marketing and PR pros on LinkedIn, and it's an important one for authors to understand. Companies hire influencers with the goal of gaining visibility with the influencer's audience.

It's no secret that a small percentage of authors make an actual living from book sales alone. According to BookScan, which tracks most bookstore sales, the average book sells less than 200 copies in a year and 1,000 copies in its lifetime. These numbers are certainly discouraging, but you're reading this book to ensure you find the tools and motivation to exceed the industry averages.

With all of this in mind, and if making money is a top goal for you, it's essential to find more ways to generate revenue *around* your book. You might do this by writing additional books. Each time you release a book, you have an opportunity to attract past readers. And a new book release tends to inspire sales of backlist titles (books you previously released).

You can also choose to sell related products and services to your audience, conduct paid speaking engagements, acquire corporate sponsorships, or generate advertising revenue as a result of having a large tribe of followers.

Corporate sponsorships can bring lucrative deals for influencers. It's not uncommon for companies to pay $1,000 to $2,500 to sponsor a single blog post, or $2,500 to $5,000 to sponsor a webinar. Sponsorships can include all kinds of promotional activities, from video endorsements to sponsored emails, and long-term contracts for influencers can reach well into the six-figure range.

Sponsorship agreements for authors are similar to those that professional athletes and celebrities have with big companies like Nike, Aveeno, and Chase bank. Celebrities are paid to endorse products and services by wearing the product, appearing in commercials, or talking about the product publicly. While celebrity contracts tend to land in the seven-figure range, and authors and influencers may fall in the five- to six-figure range, the premise is the same. Celebrities are sponsored because of their influence. As an author, you can build your influence and create lucrative sponsorship opportunities.

The required size of your audience will depend on who you serve. For a small niche topic, an audience of ten thousand people could be impressive to sponsors, but for a broader topic, you will probably need to reach more than fifty thousand to gain attention.

Adopt the Ultimate Equation: Content + Community

Influencers all have one thing in common: they share content to engage their communities. Whether it's Lady Gaga sharing pictures from her latest concert rehearsal, recipes from popular home chef Ree Drummond, how-to tips from author James Clear, or lyrical poems by the brilliant Amanda Gorman, we become fans because we like the content.

Content marketing is the act of sharing information for marketing purposes. By providing value to your target audience, you can inspire them to become part of your Tribe of Influence. Here are some top content marketing strategies to consider:

- Writing blog posts—your own or guest posts on other sites
- Hosting a podcast or serving as a guest on podcasts
- Speaking to groups in-person or online

- Sharing content on social media
- Engaging with group members, online or in-person
- Writing a column for an industry publication or blog
- Sharing videos on YouTube
- Hosting free webinars or online events
- Giving away free reports and other content that grow your email list

While building an audience can sound daunting, it is the absolute best way to ensure continuous book sales for the long haul and to build a thriving career as a thought leader in your field. Bulk sales opportunities can eventually run dry, and paid ads can run their course and become less effective. ***When you cultivate a community of fans using effective content marketing methods, you can ensure sales momentum will continue to grow.***

So, instead of spending your Saturdays driving to and from a bookstore, sitting at a table, and hoping for a handful of book sales, invest your precious time in cultivating your tribe. It's a process that won't happen overnight, but your efforts can lead to a lucrative, satisfying, and long-lasting author career.

Own Your Niche

When setting out to launch your book into the world, you will be faced with plenty of competition. There are millions of book titles available today, which means that book categories are jam-packed with options for readers. At the moment of this writing, here are the total number of titles listed on Amazon for various nonfiction book categories:

- Biography and Memoir: 507,000
- Business and Money: 1.8 million
- Computers and Technology: 415,000
- Health, Fitness, and Dieting: 676,000
- Parenting and Relationship: 230,000
- Reference: 2.8 million
- Religion and Spirituality: 1.3 million
- Self-Help: 423,000

Of course, there are also subcategories on Amazon, which have less competition. Under Business and Money, here are some subcategories and the number of titles listed in each:

- Business and Money > Marketing and Sales > Advertising: 20,000
- Business and Money > Marketing and Sales > Biographies: 13,000
- Business and Money > Marketing and Sales > Sales and Selling: 16,000
- Business and Money > Small Business and Entrepreneurship > Home-Based: 11,000
- Business and Money > Small Business and Entrepreneurship > Marketing: 3,000

As you can see, even the smallest subcategories have tremendous competition. This means it is imperative you find a way to make your book stand out against the rest, and the best way to do that is to get clear about your audience and carve out a niche.

For example, you could:

- Write another general financial-planning guide, which will have dozens or even hundreds of competing titles. Or, your book could be aimed at providing strategies for single moms, college kids, or baby boomers getting a late start on planning.
- Write a book on parenting, or you could write a book about parenting for single dads, parenting special needs children, or parenting through the challenging teen years.
- Write a book on how to live a happier life, or you could write about how to thrive after divorce, how to enjoy life while living with diabetes, or ways to live happier on a budget.

The same rules apply to narrative nonfiction and memoir. Instead of marketing your memoir to the masses, consider focusing on a theme from the memoir—like how you have managed to live a full life with a disability. Then, you can target your marketing efforts toward others with disabilities.

If one of the themes from your memoir is about your experience in military service, focus on military families or historians. If you have overcome adversity of any kind, others can relate. Find those who do relate because they will be the easiest audience to connect with.

If you're writing a history book about the town where you grew up, it will appeal to those who have lived there in the past, as well as those who live there now and in the future. It may also be of interest to residents of the state and local historical societies.

While we all want our books to appeal to the largest audience possible, choosing a niche focus doesn't mean that others outside your chosen focus won't read it. Instead, it allows your book to stand out in the eyes of its ideal target readers. Claiming a niche can allow your book to rise to the top of a busy category, build readership, establish you as an authority and influencer in your subject matter, and ultimately sell more books.

And by the way, if your book is already written and published, it's not too late to carve out a niche. Simply shift your marketing efforts toward your ideal audience.

EXERCISE: Questions to Help Clarify Your Niche Audience

Who can relate to my book and the information I share?

_____

_____

_____

_____

Who else has been through similar experiences?

_____

_____

_____

_____

Who am I passionate about wanting to inspire, teach, help, or entertain?

_____

_____

_____

_____

What audience can I find from my personal background? (Do you have a background in military service? Have you been a kids sports coach? Did you work in high tech or health care? Are you a schoolteacher, dog walker, or a federal employee? All of these can be niche audiences of their own.)

_____

_____

_____

_____

Are there clients or groups of people I've worked with in the past who could be considered a targeted niche?

_____

_____

_____

_____

Are there people/clients I do NOT want to target or work with?

_____

_____

_____

_____

Where do I want my books to be sold? For example, if you are aiming at colleges, your audience might be young finance professionals or people starting out in the tech industry.

_____

_____

_____

_____

Where do I want to speak?

_____

_____

_____

_____

How do I want to make a difference in the world?

_____

_____

_____

_____

What information is missing in my space?

_____

_____

_____

_____

How could I bridge a gap or bring something new to my audience?

_____

_____

_____

_____

EXERCISE: Claim Your Target Audience

Ideally, you should begin by focusing on one primary audience. However, if you want to reach several audiences, list them here. Just keep in mind that your marketing efforts should clearly address the needs and challenges of your *primary* target audience. If you try to appeal to too many people, you miss the benefits of carving out that niche for yourself.

Primary audience: _____

Secondary audience: _____

Additional audience: _____

How to Locate Your Target Audience

Once you know who you want to reach, every bit of your marketing messaging should speak to them. You also need to determine how you will reach them, which means finding out where they spend their time. Research opportunities by answering the following questions:

What blogs and websites do they visit?

_____

_____

_____

_____

What print publications do they read?

_____

_____

_____

_____

What podcasts do they listen to?

_____

_____

_____

_____

What YouTube channels do they follow?

_____

_____

_____

_____

Who are the top five authors they follow?

_____

_____

_____

_____

What trade associations do they belong to?

_____

_____

_____

_____

What conferences do they attend?

_____

_____

_____

_____

What social media networks do they frequent?

_____

_____

_____

_____

Who do they follow on their favorite social media networks?

_____

_____

_____

_____

What groups do they belong to on Facebook, LinkedIn, or elsewhere?

_____

_____

_____

_____

Where else can I connect with them?

_____

_____

_____

_____

By the way, if you're interested in learning more about the power of a niche audience, I wrote a whole book on this subject, _Own Your Niche: Hype-Free Internet Marketing Tactics to Establish Authority in Your Field and Promote Your Service-Based Business._

EXERCISE: Conduct a Competitive Analysis

Though this step should be done before you even write your book, it is also helpful to know the competitive landscape before you launch your book. You should understand what your top competition will be, who the audience is for those books, and how your book is different. This allows you to identify your book's advantages in the marketplace.

Note that you can often find the key selling points for a book in its description and table of contents. Your competitive analysis can also help you narrow the focus of your target audience, since this research may uncover an unmet need or opportunity in your marketplace.

Identify at least three titles that will compete with yours, along with the categories they are listed in on Amazon. Hint: check the categories for the print AND Kindle editions for each title since the categories may vary for each edition. You will want to keep track of these categories for use later.

Also review the websites and social media platforms for each author. What do they do well? What could you do better?

Title:_____

Author:_____

Target audience(s):_____

Amazon categories:

_____

_____

_____

_____

Key selling points:

_____

_____

_____

_____

How is your book different or better?

_____

_____

_____

_____

_____

Author website and social media links:

_____

_____

_____

_____

What services are offered? What is the social media strategy? What is being done well? What could you do better?

_____

_____

_____

_____

Title:_____

Author:_____

Target audience(s):_____

Amazon categories:

_____

_____

_____

_____

Key selling points:

_____

_____

_____

_____

How is your book different or better?

_____

_____

_____

_____

Author website and social media links:

_____

_____

_____

_____

What services are offered? What is the social media strategy? What is being done well? What could you do better?

_____

_____

_____

_____

Title:_____

Author:_____

Target audience(s):_____

Amazon categories:

_____

_____

_____

_____

Key selling points:

_____

_____

_____

_____

How is your book different or better?

_____

_____

_____

_____

Author website and social media links:

_____

_____

_____

_____

What services are offered? What is the social media strategy? What is being done well? What could you do better?

_____

_____

_____

_____

Make Your Book Shine—Or Waste Your Time

All the marketing in the world won't matter if your book doesn't exceed expectations of your readers. Your very first step before you even think about marketing is to aim to write a book that readers like enough to enthusiastically recommend to their friends. *This is a crucial part of the process.* Please do not release your book if you cut corners on editing or production, rushed it to market, or know it's lacking in some way. Wait until it's the absolute best book it can be.

I recommend reading popular books in your genre—the top sellers—and notice what makes them worthy of recommending to friends. It's usually because the book moved you in some way. For a memoir, you might feel deeply touched by a well-told story or find it funny and entertaining. Consider some examples:

- *Love Warrior* by Glennon Doyle shares a deeply personal account of Doyle's efforts to save her struggling marriage. It's raw and vulnerable and shares unexpected stories that make you feel like you're peeking behind the curtain of a neighbor's marriage.
- *10% Happier* by Dan Harris details the journalist's journey through anxiety and depression, starting with an on-air panic attack. It's written with wit and insight that makes you feel like you're connecting with a relatable friend.

For prescriptive nonfiction, rave reviews happen when a book inspires readers, makes a difficult task look easy, or entertains readers with humor. Consider the following examples:

- *Atomic Habits: An Easy & Proven Way to Build Good Habits & Break Bad Ones* by James Clear is compulsively readable because the author makes challenging topics—like getting in a routine to go to the gym each morning—sound easy and achievable. The book offers a fresh perspective on how to build and cultivate habits and leaves the reader feeling like he can accomplish just about anything. (I refer to it as *Atomic Goals* when recommending it to my own friends because it's truly inspiring.)
- *You Are a Badass: How to Stop Doubting Your Greatness and Start Living an Awesome Life* by Jen Sincero propelled its way up all the best sellers lists because the author is an exceptional storyteller. The book didn't appeal to me initially, but after at least four friends recommended it, I downloaded the audio version and was charmed by her wit. (And again, the power of recommendation reveals itself. This starts with writing a recommendation-worthy book.)

While dishing out advice on how to live a more fulfilling and successful life, Sincero weaves in real-world stories about her clients along with laugh-out-loud vignettes from her own life. Her personal stories are self-deprecating, making fun of her years of hustling to pay the rent, yet also vulnerable and inspiring because she ultimately figures out how to build her own successful business.

The icing on the cake is her raw sense of humor. Sincero evokes laughter and the book is loaded with F-bombs and four-letter-word grenades that aren't commonly found in self-help books. While she offers some run-of-the-mill self-help advice, it's elevated by the art of entertaining storytelling along with inspiration to make the reader feel he can reach his own goals.

Bottom line here: be sure to weave in stories and examples that bring your book to life, add humor when possible, and deliver inspiration to readers. You can always hire experienced editors and book coaches to assist. Without a buzz-worthy book, all your efforts will leave you spinning in circles.

Download Bonus Items

You can download and print many of the exercises and checklists featured in this workbook along with additional bonus content here: http://workbookbonus.com.

Quick Productivity Tips

- Keep a running to-do list and each day choose to check off at least three tasks that move you closer toward reaching your goals.

- Don't check email until you've accomplished a few goals for the day. Most email can wait a bit or be checked just once or twice a day.

- Beware of going down the social media rabbit hole. Set a timer so you only spend ten minutes on your social networks and visit them just two or three times per day.

- When writing your manuscript, if you need to look something up, create a system to make note in your manuscript and come back to it later. I mark areas in my manuscript with "xxx" so I can search for them later and fill in the missing content. Checking facts on the internet and other distractions make it challenging to get back in the flow.

- Pay attention to where you can carve out a little extra time for book marketing tasks each day. Maybe you don't need to watch a full hour of news in the morning. Perhaps you could set your alarm and get up a little earlier or promise yourself you will put in thirty minutes of effort before settling in to watch Netflix at night.

CHAPTER 2

Cultivate Your Community (Tribe of Influence)

A community is a group of people with a common interest. Communities can be formed by people living in the same neighborhood, sharing similar interests or beliefs, or participating in an activity or sport together. A community can exist in person or online, though an online community can potentially reach far more people.

When the founders of EmazingLights appeared on an episode of NBC's *Shark Tank*, they demonstrated how their LED-covered gloves are used by people who love to dance—a trend called "gloving." Instead of spending countless dollars in advertising to sell one pair of gloves at a time, these smart business owners founded an association for gloving enthusiasts where members can learn about gloving competitions and events and connect with each other. This niche product company built their own tribe, and tremendous success inevitably followed.

Peloton has gained massive popularity in recent years, largely due to the community behind the brand. Peloton exercise bikes, which cost upward of $2,500, are connected to online classes, and are even set up to send you text reminders that it's time to get some exercise—something traditional exercise bikes don't do.

In 2015, a Peloton member launched a Facebook group to connect with other Peloton users. A year later, the company seized the opportunity to take over the group and cultivate its tribe of users. Today, the private Facebook community, which is only open to active Peloton customers, boasts nearly half a million members. This undoubtedly cultivates far more brand loyalty by bringing faithful users together to bond over shared goals, not to mention the added benefit for new Peloton buyers who want to be part of the community.

A website can transform into a community, and a fun example of this is <u>BackyardChickens.com</u>, a site offering resources for people raising chickens in their backyard. Most visitors come to the site for its built-in community forum, allowing the chicken-raising community at large to discuss all-things-chicken. From deciding how to design coops to the care and feeding of these feathered pets, this online community serves an eager niche of website visitors and attracts an incredible amount of website traffic: *more than one million unique visitors each month*. Traffic numbers like that mean tremendous revenue in advertising alone. It also led site owner Rob Ludlow to be asked to coauthor *Raising Chickens for Dummies*.

Communities have traditionally been established by individuals, which is a missed opportunity for all kinds of companies. Imagine the possibilities:

- A printing company that creates a forum for customers to brainstorm and share their creative design ideas.
- A travel company that hosts a discussion group for European adventure-seekers.
- A software company that hosts online events for users to learn and connect.
- A brick-and-mortar retailer that hosts monthly workshops for customers.
- A law firm or accounting firm or other service-based business that hosts a discussion forum where members can get their questions answered.

Indeed, there are countless ways to cultivate a community and build tremendous brand loyalty. How can you establish yourself as an influencer and form a community of your own?

Find a Need for Community

Since 2006, I have been speaking at writers' conferences about book marketing and publishing, and what I've always found to be so disappointing is the lack of attention paid to those of us who write nonfiction. Most writers' groups and events cater to fiction and children's book writers, and sometimes memoir writers get a little love. I have never understood why nonfiction is so widely ignored.

To address this challenge, I launched the first Nonfiction Writers Conference in 2010. It was delivered entirely online over three days, featuring live speakers and Q&A with attendees, just like an in-person conference. It was well-received, so we've continued ever since. Each year attendees would ask how they could keep in touch after the event was over. I listened and ultimately responded by launching the Nonfiction Authors Association in 2013, and our community began taking shape quickly.

Then my husband died unexpectedly five months after the Nonfiction Authors Association was born, and I was devastated. In all honestly, I essentially checked out for a year, letting our team manage most details and only contributing a small amount of content and the tiniest amount of effort. Despite my lack of engagement, our community grew. And grew and grew and grew. You are reading this book because our community let me know they needed this content in the form of a book and companion course.

Today we have members from around the globe. We host a year-round book awards program, weekly podcast interviews, a private forum for members, online courses, and so much more. I never imagined how big we would get so quickly, and I am deeply grateful. It is also personally rewarding to create something from the ground up and know it makes an impact.

As an author and expert in your own field, you can create your own community. It doesn't have to be a massive undertaking like starting your own association. It could be as simple as creating a group on Facebook or LinkedIn. Or adding a forum to your website for discussions. Or hosting live events online where you connect with members of your community on a regular basis.

There is tremendous power in community, plus the opportunity to make a difference. And members of a community can be your book readers for the long-haul.

EXERCISE: Consider Creating Your Own Community

What kinds of communities exist for your target audience today? Identify trade associations, Meetup groups, and online groups where your audience spends time.

_____

_____

_____

_____

What is missing in your community? How are they not yet being served?

_____

_____

_____

_____

What are some ways you could build a supportive community for your tribe?

_____

_____

_____

_____

Build Your Platform with Your Tribe of Influence

In the publishing industry, we hear the word "platform" constantly. Publishers want authors to build a platform, which can sound intimidating and even overwhelming. But a "platform" simply means an audience. You may not realize this, but your current platform is probably bigger than you think.

The fact is that you know more people than you realize, and when you spend time digging into your contacts, you might just strike gold. Your Tribe of Influence starts with people you already know—people who can help you spread the word about your books. They may also help you build your author business in ways you haven't yet imagined.

Here are some of the ways your Tribe of Influence can help:

- **Book sales** – Purchase copies of your book during your launch campaign and beyond.
- **Endorsements** – Well-known authors in your genre can provide testimonials for your book cover or contribute a foreword.

- **Reviews** – Post reviews on Amazon, Goodreads, Barnes and Noble, etc.
- **Beta reader support** – Provide editorial feedback, reviews, and promotion support.
- **Industry promotion** – Recommend your book in an industry blog, newsletter, or print publication.
- **Guest blog posts** – Publish guest blog posts or book excerpts that you provide.
- **Social media** – Share book-promotion messages across social media platforms.
- **Podcast** – Feature you on an industry podcast, teleseminar, or webinar event.
- **Speaking opportunities** – Invite you to speak at a meeting, event, or conference.
- **Bulk sales** – Buy copies of your book in bulk to distribute to event attendees, staff, etc.
- **Sponsorship** – Contribute to your book tour or campaign by donating funds or in-kind items, such as printing services or banners, in exchange for promotion.
- **Connections and introductions** – In addition to asking your tribe for the above support, you can also ask them, *"Who do you know who can help?"* Perhaps a former client has a personal connection with a trade association, nonprofit, or an event planner for an opportunity for you to speak at an upcoming conference. You'll never know unless you ask!
- **Community** – Leverage your Tribe of Influence to begin seeding your own community to serve your audience. Ask them to join and participate and support your efforts.

Identify Your Tribe of Influence

I wholeheartedly believe that every author should complete the Tribe of Influence exercise detailed below. This is important whether you already have a platform or not, because you might be surprised by how many people you know who can help support your book and your overall author-career goals. And in addition to those you already know personally, there are many other people you can connect with to support your book launch.

Consider the following people:

- **Friends and family** – Your closest family and friends may be able to connect you with people who can help you accomplish your goals. However, don't rely on them to be your primary source for book reviews. It's important to earn reviews from unbiased readers.
- **Fellow authors** – Authors in your industry who have a large platform can have a big impact on book sales simply by recommending your book to their own tribes via social media or their own email lists.
- **Influencers in your target industry** – This includes bloggers, podcast hosts, YouTubers, and social media stars.
- **Trade association leaders and members** – Trade associations that reach your target audience can be a powerful place to build your tribe. Do you know someone who can recommend you as a speaker at an annual conference or a monthly meeting? Or help you contribute guest content to the association blog or newsletter?

- **Online groups** – If you participate in groups that reach your target readers, ask the group owner if you can share book announcements or invite beta readers from the group. Facebook and LinkedIn groups that focus on your niche can be a fantastic place to build your readership.
- **Current and past coworkers** – Perhaps you worked with someone ten years ago who now organizes big corporate events or is a leader in your industry. Reach out to these types of connections.
- **Current and past clients** – If someone has already enjoyed working with you in some way, they will likely be glad to support your new book launch and related goals.
- **Past readers** – Readers who liked your previous book(s) will certainly be interested in your next one.
- **Social media followers** – Think of social media as a way to cultivate your author-tribe and build relationships with raving fans.
- **Email list subscribers** – If you're not yet building an email list, you should be. This is hands down one of the best marketing tools you can have. Social media is passive and time-based, but email lands in the recipients' inboxes and is far more likely to be read.
- **Corporate and nonprofit contacts** – Who do you know at corporations or nonprofits that could connect you with speaking opportunities, consulting opportunities, or bulk book sales?
- **Media pros** – This includes journalists, reporters, editors, and producers on a local or national level and those who cover topics related to your book.

TRIBE OF INFLUENCE

EXERCISE: Build Your Tribe of Influence Lists

Spend some quiet time brainstorming lists of people you can contact and ask for support. You can download specially formatted Tribe of Influence worksheets here: http://workbookbonus.com.

Review copy recipients and beta readers:

- ☐ Industry influencers
- ☐ Mailing list subscribers
- ☐ Past readers
- ☐ Clients, peers, family, and friends
- ☐ Members of online groups
- ☐ Members of trade associations
- ☐ Media professionals
- ☐ Book reviewers
- ☐ Book review sites
- ☐ Trade association staff
- ☐ Any person or company mentioned in your book

Book endorsements:

- ☐ Authors in your genre, including competitors
- ☐ Celebrities
- ☐ Corporate executives and other top professionals in your industry

Industry influencers who reach your target audience:

- ☐ Bloggers
- ☐ Podcasters
- ☐ Fellow authors
- ☐ YouTubers
- ☐ Association executives
- ☐ Social media stars

Media pros:

- ☐ Reporters
- ☐ Editors
- ☐ Producers
- ☐ Hosts
- ☐ Local and national media outlets
- ☐ Industry-specific media outlets (trade publications)

Groups where your target readers spend time:

- ☐ Trade associations
- ☐ Alumni groups
- ☐ Meetup groups
- ☐ Online groups (Facebook, LinkedIn, other forums)
- ☐ Nonprofits
- ☐ Sports organizations
- ☐ Religious/spiritual organizations

Connections to speaking engagement opportunities:

- ☐ Association executives
- ☐ Association board members or volunteers
- ☐ Event planners
- ☐ Corporate contacts
- ☐ Trade show organizers

Potential sponsors and bulk buyers:

- ☐ Corporations
- ☐ Nonprofits
- ☐ Trade associations
- ☐ Past clients
- ☐ Current clients
- ☐ Schools
- ☐ Spiritual organizations

Influencers

Locate bloggers and social media stars who reach your target audience and look to see if they post book reviews, accept guest blog posts, conduct interviews, or host book-giveaway contests.

Contact Name	Website and Email	What is your Ask?

Media Contacts

Build a media list or purchase a list from a resource such as <u>Cision.com</u>. Your media list should begin with local print, radio, and television since local media attention is often the easiest to get. Then expand your list to include media outlets across the country—especially niche media outlets like trade publications that reach your target audience.

Media Outlet	Contact Name	Email Address

Podcasts

Research podcasts to find programs where you should be a guest. Look for their guest submission guidelines (most need guests).

Contact Name	Website and Email	What is your Ask?

Trade Associations

What associations do your potential readers belong to? Visit association websites and look for opportunities. Can you contribute posts to their blog, write for their newsletter or magazine, apply to speak at local meetings or a national event, or even join their board of directors?

Contact Name	Website and Email	What is your Ask?

Speaking Opportunities

Who could get you booked to speak at an event? This can include trade association executives or volunteers/staff, event organizers, and corporate contacts.

Group Name	Contact Name	Email

Bulk Book Buyers and Sponsors

Potential bulk buyers and sponsors can include past clients, corporations, associations, nonprofits, schools, and others who might purchase larger quantities of your books.

Company Name	Contact Name	Email

Recommended Resources and Contributors

List any person or company that you recommend as a resource in your book. You should notify each of them prior to your book release and mail a review copy. They may in turn show their appreciation by spreading the word about your book. The same is true for anyone who contributed a quote or interview for your book.

Name	Email	Mailing Address

Once you populate your lists, your next step is to begin reaching out. Some people on your list should be contacted individually, while others can be contacted in groups. For example, you could reach out to members of an online forum you belong to and ask them to join your beta reader team. Or you might reach out to a past client who works for a local nonprofit and ask for help getting booked as a speaker at their next meeting.

Keep in mind that people you know want to support you. Sometimes all you have to do is ask.

Reminder: You can download a pre-formatted spreadsheet to begin building your lists here: http://workbookbonus.com.

CHAPTER 3

Master Your Content Marketing

When you have a deep understanding of what matters to your audience, you can gain their loyalty by educating, inspiring, or entertaining them. Providing valuable content is one of the best ways to cultivate a long-term relationship with a loyal audience.

Let's say you've authored a memoir about your journey through divorce, and your target audience is women going through divorce with children at home. Their needs and challenges would likely be managing finances, locating childcare, planning for the future, and coping with the emotional aftermath. Once you identify these pain points, then the content you create, and all your marketing efforts, can help address their challenges.

For history, science, or other narrative nonfiction books, you may not address pain points or challenges, but you can identify the interests of readers. Here are some examples:

- A book about the history of the town where you live—focus on sharing a variety of interesting local history stories and interviewing people about their own experiences living there.
- A collection of essays about serving in the military—focus on providing support or tips for active military families or for veterans.
- A funny story about life with your dog—stay with the humor theme and offer amusing content that easily gets passed around social media networks. Or focus on heartwarming dog stories, tips for dog care, or any number of animal-related themes.

What are the needs, challenges, and interests of your target audience? Identify as many as you can. If you have difficulty with this exercise, you may need to survey your audience. You will use this data later for crafting your marketing plans, and—if you plan to further monetize your efforts—for developing companion products and services.

EXERCISE: Identify Audience Challenges, Needs, and Pain Points

Challenges/Needs/Pain Points/Interests	
Ex: Locating allergen-free recipes	
Ex: Interested in fact-based information	

Convey Reader Benefits

Conveying the benefits of your book is essential to converting browsers into buyers. Benefits should address readers' pain points and challenges, or the interests you have identified. These benefits are essential to helping you write effective jacket copy and build content marketing strategies that speak to the needs of your audience.

Here's a brief excerpt from Elizabeth Gilbert's jacket copy for *Big Magic: Creative Living Beyond Fear*:

> She asks us to embrace our curiosity and let go of needless suffering. She shows us how to tackle what we most love, and how to face down what we most fear. She discusses the attitudes, approaches, and habits we need in order to live our most creative lives.

If you're interested in living a more creative life, the above copy likely resonates with you.

As we've discussed, narrative nonfiction is more about how you will entertain your reader. Here's an excerpt from Elizabeth Gilbert's memoir *Eat, Pray, Love: One Woman's Search for Everything Across Italy, India, and Indonesia*:

> This wise and rapturous book is the story of how she left behind all these outward marks of success and set out to explore three different aspects of her nature, against the backdrop of three different cultures: pleasure in Italy, devotion in India, and on the Indonesian island of Bali, a balance between worldly enjoyment and divine transcendence.

The subtleties of this description appeal to a target audience of women who feel slightly dissatisfied with life, despite "having it all." A target audience has been defined and addressed in this copy.

EXERCISE: Identify Reader Benefits

What benefits will readers gain from your book? How will their lives be improved in some way? List your answers below.

Reader Benefits
Ex. Help them overcome fear of cold calling so they can increase sales.
Ex. Discover ways to keep their children safe from internet predators.
Ex. Enjoy a laugh-out-loud journey...

Write a Book Description That Sells

The back cover is where you convince readers to buy. There is a limited amount of space on the back of your book, so it's essential to make every word count. The goal is to entice your target audience and convince them to purchase your book. Following are some guidelines.

Research Other Books

Start by reading the jacket copy on other books, especially from books in the same genre as yours. Find out how other authors position their books and what benefits they highlight. This will help you get a better understanding of what jacket copy should look like. It can also help you identify ways that your book is different from your competitors' books, which you'll want to emphasize when writing your copy. You can do much of this research on Amazon, since most book listings feature the back-cover copy or even an expanded version of the back-cover copy.

Write Three Versions

It is helpful to craft three versions of your copy:

- A longer version (full page), which can be used on your website and for online sales copy.
- Three paragraphs (maximum) that will be used for your book jacket. I also recommend including a bulleted list of benefits within your three paragraphs.
- A captivating single-paragraph description.

It is often easiest to start by writing a longer version, and then trim that down to your book jacket copy, and from that craft a powerful single paragraph. Note that it is important to draw readers in by identifying them directly, and then help them relate to the solutions offered by your book. Starting with a question can also help readers relate. Here are some real-world examples of compelling opening paragraphs:

> Advances in behavioral sciences are giving us an ever better understanding of how our brains work, why we make the choices we do, and what it takes for us to be at our best. But it has not always been easy to see how to apply these insights in the real world—until now.
>
> —*How to Have a Good Day: Harness the Power of Behavioral Science to Transform Your Working Life* by Caroline Webb

> Anarchy is coming. Decentralization is accelerating, and technology is facilitating the trend. Nobody trusts traditional institutions or authority figures anymore. Bitcoin, open source, Uber, social media, and the Arab Spring are all examples of anarchy in

action. Tomorrow's leaders need to understand these trends if they wish to thrive in a decentralized economy.

—*Anarchy, Inc.: Profiting in a Decentralized World with Artificial Intelligence and Blockchain* by Patrick Schwerdtfeger

Do you feel frustrated because you can't seem to finish every item on your daily to-do lists? Do you feel discouraged because you're not effectively managing your workload and responsibilities at your office and home? If so, it's not your fault.

—*To-Do List Formula: A Stress-Free Guide to Creating To-Do Lists that Work!* by Damon Zahariades

For narrative nonfiction, the jacket copy needs to pique the interest of readers and perhaps give them something they can relate to.

Is it possible for humans to discover the key to happiness through a bigger-than-life, bad-boy dog? Just ask the Grogans.

—*Marley & Me: Life and Love with the World's Worst Dog* by John Grogan

Candy Montgomery and Betty Gore had a lot in common: They sang together in the Methodist church choir, their daughters were best friends, and their husbands had good jobs working for technology companies in the north Dallas suburbs known as Silicon Prairie. But beneath the placid surface of their seemingly perfect lives, both women simmered with unspoken frustrations and unanswered desires.

—*Evidence of Love: A True Story of Passion and Death in the Suburbs* by John Bloom and Jim Atkinson

Which is more dangerous, a gun or a swimming pool? What do schoolteachers and sumo wrestlers have in common? Why do drug dealers still live with their moms? How much do parents really matter? How did the legalization of abortion affect the rate of violent crime? These may not sound like typical questions for an economist to ask. But Steven D. Levitt is not a typical economist. He is a much-heralded scholar who studies the riddles of everyday life—from cheating and crime to sports and child-rearing—and whose conclusions turn conventional wisdom on its head.

—*Freakonomics: A Rogue Economist Explores the Hidden Side of Everything* by Steven D. Levitt and Stephen J. Dubner

Focus on Benefits

For prescriptive nonfiction, you should highlight benefits that the reader will gain, ideally in a bulleted list following the introductory paragraph. To uncover the benefits in your book, identify what problems your book solves for readers. If you wrote a time management book, your benefits might look like this:

Time Management Mastery will teach you how to:

- Reclaim two hours from each day (without getting up earlier!).
- Empty that in-box once and for all—and keep it under control forever.
- Improve your productivity by 500 percent with one simple change.
- Reduce your stress by starting a simple daily habit.

Note how each item above promises to improve the reader's life in some way. This is an essential sales technique when convincing someone to buy just about any product or service, and is especially valuable for positioning your book.

For narrative nonfiction, you may not overtly list the reader benefits, but you still need to think about what's in it for the reader. Ask yourself these questions:

- How will the reader be entertained?
- What will the reader learn as a result of reading my story?
- What kind of journey will the reader be taken on?

The jacket copy for Jeannette Walls' *The Glass Castle: A Memoir,* which spent more than seven years on the *New York Times* Best Sellers list, hooks the reader by answering the questions above. See for yourself:

The Glass Castle is a remarkable memoir of resilience and redemption, and a revelatory look into a family at once deeply dysfunctional and uniquely vibrant. When sober, Jeannette's brilliant and charismatic father captured his children's imagination, teaching them physics, geology, and how to embrace life fearlessly. But when he drank, he was dishonest and destructive. Her mother was a free spirit who abhorred the idea of domesticity and didn't want the responsibility of raising a family.

Walls' description is enticing and relatable—anyone who has ever been part of a dysfunctional family will likely relate (and that's a substantial audience). It also promises to be hopeful, so that the reader will be inspired. This is the magic formula needed to make truly impactful jacket copy.

End with a Call to Action

Finish up your copy with a strong call to action. That means that you are going to ask the reader to make the purchase. Here are some examples:

- If you're ready to take back control of your life, you need this book!
- Never before has anyone revealed so many inside secrets to the industry. Can you afford not to buy this book?
- This book will show you exactly what it takes to lose 10 pounds in 30 days—so don't waste another moment!
- Don't miss this opportunity to learn the proven system to make more money while working fewer hours. This book will change your life!

For historical books, memoir, and narrative nonfiction, your call to action will be subtle. In the example above from Jeannette Walls, the final sentence draws in the reader, with the goal of making the reader want to buy the book:

> *The Glass Castle* is truly astonishing—a memoir permeated by the intense love of a peculiar but loyal family.

If this is your first-time writing sales copy, you may want to hire a copywriter or an experienced editor to review your work and offer suggestions for improvement. The sales copy for your book has a *major impact* on a potential reader's decision to buy your book or move on to something else. Make sure your copy reflects the best your book has to offer.

Write a Compelling Author Bio

Your author bio tells readers who you are in relation to your book. I recommend authors include a single-paragraph bio on the book jacket, and a longer, more detailed bio in the final pages of the book.

Just as with writing your book description, you may want to start by writing a longer bio, and then trim it down to a medium-sized version, followed by a short version. You can also publish these on your website.

Before you write your bio, poke around similar titles on Amazon to read bios of other authors and get a feel for what works and what doesn't work.

Ideally, your bio should highlight details that relate to your authority in your subject matter. If you've written a scientific research guide, highlight any experience, degrees, or special credentials that relate to your work. You could share awards or honors you have received, too. Mentioning your three chihuahuas and your addiction to reality TV isn't exactly relevant. However, sometimes personal details can also help the reader connect to your human side, so be thoughtful about what details you share.

In the shortest version, it's best to stick to the details of your bio that will be most relevant to your readers' needs. There is more flexibility in the longer version of your bio, which should also be relevant, yet can highlight some personal details. If you want to note the city where you live, your volunteer role at your favorite nonprofit, and even your passion for disc golf, do it after you have established your credibility.

A big opportunity that too many authors miss is to share a call to action, which I defined earlier. At the end of your short bio, be sure to add a line like this:

> Learn more at AnnieAuthorsAwesomeWebsite.com.

At the end of your longer bio, you could also mention services you offer. Here are some examples:

> Annie Author consults with Fortune 500 companies. If you're interested in working with her, you can learn more about her consulting services here: <website link>.

> Need a speaker for your next event? Annie Author is an experienced and engaging keynote speaker. Visit her speaker page here: <link>.

> Quantity discounts are available on copies of this book. Contact the publisher to inquire: <email address>.

> Want to learn more? My online course will help you put the concepts from this book into action: <link>.

The point here is that you can put in any kind of call to action you want, and I encourage you to do so. Readers may love your book, get to the end, and not even realize that you could be hired as a consultant or speaker at their next event. Plant the seed!

EXERCISE: Write Your Jacket Copy and Author Bio

Book description

- ☐ Research sales copy from similar books.
- ☐ Write long sales copy (full page).
- ☐ Write medium sales copy for book jacket (three paragraphs).
- ☐ Write single-paragraph book description.

Author bio

- ☐ Read other author bios to get a feel for styles and content.
- ☐ Write a longer version first. This can include an extensive career history or details about your life that relate to your book.

☐ Open with your name, job title (if relevant), and title of your book. "Annie Author is a neuroscientist and the award-winning author of *An Inside Look at the Brains of Hamsters, Cats, and Armadillos.*"

☐ Include details about degrees or special credentials you have that relate to the book.

☐ Include personal details after you've highlighted the credibility-building content. You can endear readers by sharing with them how you volunteer for a favorite cause, the status of your family, or where you live.

☐ Add some extra personality by throwing in a couple of fun or humorous details. "Annie Author won the 2019 hot-dog-eating contest at the Bower County Fair. She hasn't been able to eat another hot dog since her victory."

☐ Keep a document with your bios handy so that you can quickly copy and paste them as needed. You will do this many times as an author and influencer.

Claim Your Content Marketing Strategy

As we've already discussed, you can attract and cultivate a loyal audience by sharing compelling content. The goal is to build a relationship that not only leads to book sales but creates fans that stay with you for the long-term. Content marketing should ideally begin before the launch of your book and continue for as long as you want to grow your author business. This is how influencers are born—by marketing content that serves their audiences.

Avoid Random Acts of Content

You've probably heard the advice to leverage social media, blogging, podcasting, and other content marketing strategies as a tool for growing your author business. However, when you do this without getting clear about the needs, challenges, and interests of your target audience, these efforts usually fall flat.

Let's take for example Joe Schmoe (not a real person) who authored a book, and blogs about, backyard farming. Joe is passionate about his topic. He converted his modest backyard into a thriving source of food for his family, and he aims to help others do the same. Despite his passion and enthusiasm, his audience isn't growing.

To date, Joe's blog contains several dozen posts. Here are some examples of his titles and topics:

- Check out my tomato harvest
- Memories made on our family vacation
- Why I like backyard gardening
- See all the salads I made this week
- Where are the helpers at the hardware store?

Now, imagine you're interested in backyard gardening. Would the above titles appeal to you? Would they make you want to click on these posts? Or subscribe and visit the blog again and again?

The biggest mistake Joe is making—and one that so many others make with content marketing—is that he's not considering what his audience cares about. If I'm getting ready to convert my backyard into a mini farm and I stumble on Joe's site, seeing photos of his tomatoes or reading about his family vacation offers no value to me. It doesn't address my challenges or improve my life in any way. So, I will move on, and find one of the many other blogs that can meet my needs.

Here are some better blog post titles that Joe could use:

- 10 Steps to Getting Started with Backyard Farming
- How to Create a No-Fail Watering Schedule for Your Backyard Farm
- 5 Tips for a Hearty Lettuce Harvest
- How to Select Tomato Plants and When to Plant Them
- 3 Reasons Why Your Backyard Garden is Attracting Bugs and How to Get Rid of Them

Can you see the difference here? When Joe puts himself in the shoes of his readers, he will realize they are seeking guidance. As the expert, his readers rely on him to help them get started with gardening and overcome their backyard gardening challenges. If he simply meets these needs, his blog will begin to gain readership momentum.

Identify Content Ideas

After determining what your audience cares about, you can begin to develop content that meets their needs. Following are some types of content you can create.

How-To/Prescriptive

Prescriptive content is some of the easiest to promote online because millions of people turn to the internet to seek answers to their challenges every day. When you consider what types of questions your audience is typing into search each day, you can begin to address those needs and develop content they are seeking. Your mission here is to solve their challenges and show them ways to make life easier.

Theme Related to Book

For narrative nonfiction and memoir, children's books, fiction, and poetry, you will need to choose a theme and stick with it. Your theme might come directly from your book—or not. You could focus on the location where the book is set and share history of the city or travel tips for visitors. Or, if your book discusses an illness you overcame, sharing helpful information for others battling the illness can be a powerful strategy.

Donna Hartley has authored a series of memoirs based on events from her life, including surviving a collapsed heart valve. Today she earns a full-time living as a professional speaker covering women's health issues.

Your theme might also be totally unrelated to your book. Charmaine Hammond is a business consultant who wrote a book of lessons from her dog called *On Toby's Terms*. She reached out to her business contacts and organized a cross-country tour to promote the book by speaking at dozens of locations.

Charmaine picked up the phone and acquired sponsors for the entire trip, covering everything from the borrowed RV she traveled in and a custom promotional wrap placed around the RV, to the coffee she brewed along the way and treats she shared with Toby. Her efforts led to selling tens of thousands of copies of the book and helped her further cultivate loyal fans in her business community—which is her target audience because she offers consulting and educational services for business professionals.

Entertaining and Engaging

If you're funny, you can engage an audience through laugh-inducing videos (that may go viral!) or a blog where you write hilarious short stories. Though I always recommend picking a theme and sticking with it, being funny could possibly be your focus all on its own. Author Jeremy Greenberg is a former stand-up comic and author of over ten books about pets with titles like *Sorry I Barfed on Your Bed* and *Sorry I Pooped in Your Shoe*. He writes hilarious articles for a variety of websites and publications, primarily focused on life with pets and dysfunctional families.

Storytelling is another important piece of the content pie. Great storytellers can build a following by writing for publications that reach their target audience. Without a focused theme, it may be harder to build an audience with your own site until you establish yourself by leveraging the reach that online and print publications offer. The same is true for poets. You either need a theme or you will likely need to rely on drawing interest by getting published on other platforms first.

Choose Your Content Foundation

Now that you have some idea about your content focus, you need to decide how you will produce your content. I view content strategy in three tiers:

Tier 1: Foundation

Choose at least one of these options to create a home base on your website. This gives your audience a reason to visit your site repeatedly.

- Blog
- Podcast
- Video Blog/Channel

Tier 2: Expand Your Reach

Now that you are creating content on a consistent basis, you will want to get the word out using several of these strategies.

- Email marketing
- Social media
- Speaking at events online or in person
- Hosting events online or in person
- Writing a column for a blog or publication

I strongly feel that every author needs to build an email list. It can be one of your best assets. When you participate in any social media network, you are using someone else's real estate. You can be kicked off a social media site at any time and for no good reason. And when that happens, you will have no recourse. But you will always own your list of contacts. An email service provider could kick you off the platform but they can't keep your contacts. Those belong to you. And with email, you have an engaged audience. Social media can be hit or miss since you will never be able to reach every single follower at once.

With that said, social media should play a role in your overall strategy. Think of it as a way to amplify your reach. When you create blog posts or podcast episodes, you will want to let your fans know. Sharing posts or episodes on your favorite social media networks is a great way to gain visibility and attract your ideal audience.

The good news is you don't need to be on ALL of the social media networks. I recommend choosing at least two—the ones where your audience spends time—and putting effort into utilizing them to the best of your ability.

Tier 3: Advanced Marketing

If you want to take your marketing efforts to the next level, join one or more online groups that reach your target audience—or better yet, start your own.

- Online groups (Facebook, LinkedIn, or another platform)
- Discussion forum (on your website or another platform)
- Membership community

Imagine if Joe Schmoe started a community group on Facebook about backyard farming. It wouldn't be long before people would join and Joe could share his blog posts, answer questions, and encourage communication among members. After months or even years of running the group, when it's time to release Joe's next book, he would have a large, engaged community of fans.

Host an Effective Blog

If your website is hosted on the WordPress platform, it should have the ability to create a blog. A blog is essentially a collection of articles organized by categories that you define. It's important to identify categories properly when setting up your blog because categories make it easy for site visitors to locate content they're interested in. Readers don't want to sift through past posts lumped together by date. They want to quickly find blog articles based on subjects they are interested in.

Think of your blog categories like sections of your online magazine. Using our friend Joe Schmoe and his backyard farming blog as an example, here are some categories he could create:

- Getting Started with Backyard Farming
- Growing Citrus in Your Backyard
- Growing Vegetables in Your Backyard
- Backyard Farming Problems and Solutions
- Profitable Backyard Farming
- Sustainable Backyard Farming

Once his categories are defined, each of Joe's blog posts can be listed in one or more categories, making them easy for visitors to locate.

Write Captivating Titles

Blog titles are almost more important than the actual blog content because they help your target audience quickly decide whether they want to read the content—or not. The next time you're at the grocery store, look at the headlines on magazines and how they draw readers in. A good headline addresses those interests and challenges you identified for your audience. It's wise to study blog titles on popular blogs to see how they make them more enticing and then aim to do the same for your blog posts.

Develop Theme Days

Author Karl Palachuk features "SOP Fridays" on his blog at SmallBizThoughts.com. His audience knows that each week Karl will share important Standard Operating Procedures for the IT industry (his target audience). This series has been so popular that Karl turned the previous posts into a series of books.

Feature Guest Contributors

You don't have to generate all your blog content on your own. Invite others to contribute to your blog, including industry experts and peers. Once a post is featured, let the contributor know and ask them to share with their networks. To streamline the process, create submission guidelines on your site detailing what kinds of contributions you accept. You can see an example from our site here: https://nonfictionauthorsassociation.com/contribute-to-the-blog/.

Ask for Comments

One of the biggest complaints you will hear from bloggers is that it's hard to generate comments. Most visitors won't take time to leave a comment, but you can encourage them to do so by simply asking. At the bottom of each post, ask a question or simply invite readers to respond in the comment box below. It's amazing how this simple request can yield results and improve visitor time on-site and overall engagement.

Respond to Comments

One of the many benefits of a blog is that you can engage with your audience. Be sure to respond to all comments and let your audience know you are paying attention, even if you simply say, "Thank you for taking the time to post." Responding builds loyalty that brings readers back.

Comment on Other Blogs

When you write a comment on another blog, you get the opportunity to include your photo, name, and a link back to your own site. Get known within your industry by being a power contributor to industry blogs and leaving compelling comments. A good comment contributes to the conversation by adding another tip or expanding on something the blog author mentioned. Provide value and fellow blog readers will find you. (By the way, if you want your photo to appear when you comment on a blog, set up a free profile at Gravatar.com, which is where many sites collect this information.)

Promote Related Posts

At the end of each new blog post, it can be beneficial to refer readers to similar blog posts on your site. You can summarize these yourself or WordPress users can install the Yet Another Related Posts plug-in (or a similar plugin), which will automatically serve up a list of related posts, thus keeping readers engaged and on your site longer.

Hold a Contest

You can use your blog to conduct contests where one or more winners are selected. Prizes could include a copy of a book, a brief consultation with you, attendance at an event you're hosting, a gift card, or anything else your audience would find valuable. You can also enlist other companies to donate prizes.

One of the easiest ways to do this is to hold a comment contest, asking visitors to answer a question in the comments, and then select a random winner. Contests can generate lots of buzz and more importantly, website traffic. Be sure to check the latest FTC regulations for holding online contests. Some of their current guidelines indicate you must state there is no purchase required to enter, be clear about who is hosting the contest, and set clear start and end dates.

Spread the Word

Summarize your recent blog posts in your email marketing by listing the title, first paragraph, and a link to keep reading. Your recipients will appreciate the content and more will visit your site as a result. And be sure to share your posts to your social media networks. As you share helpful or interesting content on a regular basis, you should begin to establish yourself as a thought leader on your subject matter.

EXERCISE: Brainstorm Blog Topics

Spend some time identifying blog topic ideas, especially those based on the needs, challenges, and interests of your audience that you previously identified.

_____

_____

_____

_____

_____

_____

_____

_____

_____

_____

_____

_____

_____

_____

Host Your Own Podcast

A podcast is a downloadable recording that is typically delivered as a series. Most podcasts are talk-radio-style programs that feature interviews with guests, though some are narrated by one or more hosts. Listeners can download and listen to podcast recordings on their phones, computers, or other mobile devices. Newer models of cars now feature Apple CarPlay, which puts the podcast app right in the dashboard of the car (along with other popular apps). There are thousands of podcast programs produced today and some have hundreds of thousands of regular listeners.

It is relatively easy to produce your own podcast and it provides another powerful way to reach your target audience. First, be clear about who your target audience is and what kinds of content they will be interested in. Next, visit the iTunes store or Stitcher Radio and sample some podcasts to learn how they are conducted, along with what you like and don't like.

Podcast Recording Options

- You will need a good microphone to produce high quality audio. Good options include Blue Yeti and Audio-Technica.
- To record interviews remotely, you can use a conference line with Zoom to generate a quality recording. Or you can use a free service like FreeConferenceCall.com.
- If you prefer to use Skype, you can get recording services via voipcallrecording.com/ or pamela.biz/en/.

Podcast Editing Options

- Audacity is free and relatively easy to use: audacity.com.
- GarageBand is available for Mac users: apple.com/mac/garageband/.

Podcast Publishing and Distribution Options

- Note that you should have a podcast cover image designed to display with your content.
- Utilize a service to handle publishing and distribution of your episodes. Affordable options include Buzzsprout, Liberated Syndication (libsyn.com) or PodBean.com.
- Most podcasters list their shows as individual blog posts on their own websites and include show notes, which are details about what's included in the show, a list of any links or resources recommended, and a link to access the recording.

Don't forget to promote your podcasts to your audience. After posting them to your blog, you can share to your social media networks.

EXERCISE: Plan Your Podcast

Answer the following questions:

Will you release episodes daily or weekly?

_____

_____

_____

_____

Will they last thirty minutes, an hour, or another duration?

_____

_____

_____

_____

Will you interview guests or narrate your content?

_____

_____

_____

_____

What topics does your target audience care about?

_____

_____

_____

_____

If featuring guests, who do you want to invite?

_____

_____

_____

_____

What will you call your show?

_____

_____

_____

_____

Create Videos with YouTube

Did you know that YouTube is the second-largest search engine next to Google? And since Google owns YouTube, videos appear in nearly every Google search conducted. When you search for "how to change a tire" or "how to bake an apple pie," several videos will inevitably be listed in the top-ten results.

If you can be engaging on video or if you cover topics with a visual component, creating a YouTube channel could be the foundation for your content marketing strategy. Following are some tips for getting started with YouTube.

- Start with shorter videos (under five minutes) since they tend to get best results.
- Aim for funny, educational, or controversial content.
- Create a variety of videos. Formats can include:

  o Talking head—you speaking about a topic.
  o On location—shot at an event.
  o A demonstration—these are perfect for topics with a visual component, such as cooking or exercising.
  o Tutorials, such as recording a demonstration on your computer with Camtasia (software).
  o Interviews conducted in-person or via Zoom or Skype.

- Embed your videos in your blog as individual posts and then share with any other social media networks you use.
- You might consider using YouTube's advertising platform to help build a following for your video collection. The more subscribers you gain, the more chances you have to promote your books and any other products or services you offer.

EXERCISE: Plan Your Videos

Answer the following questions:

How often will you produce videos and when will you record them?

_____

_____

_____

_____

How long will your videos be? How many will you record at a time?

_____

_____

_____

_____

What topics will you cover?

_____

_____

_____

_____

What will you call your YouTube channel?

_____

_____

_____

_____

CHAPTER 4

Set Your Goals and Budget

Embarking on marketing your book can feel like you're about to traverse rough terrain up an enormous mountain in a snowstorm, after only hiking on short, flat paths on sunny days. I'm not going to tell you that marketing your book will be easy. I wish it was easy and that there were shortcuts to true success, but that just doesn't exist. There also aren't shortcuts to becoming a champion chess player, running a marathon, earning a degree, or being a parent. Any significant accomplishment in life requires effort and work. Marketing a book is no exception.

If you're persistent and willing to do the work, my hope is that this one-of-a-kind workbook will help propel your author career to a new level. I want you to set big goals and reach them, because that means that you're out there making a difference in the lives of your readers.

We are the difference-makers, the game-changers, and the passionate advocates with something to say.

If you want to make your dent in the universe, it starts with taking steps up that mountain each day. Instead of focusing on how far away the top of the mountain may be, try to focus on only your next few steps. This is how goals are won—in small, incremental steps.

Consider this: if you walked ten blocks a day, you'd walk a mile in two days. And if you kept walking ten blocks each day, you would walk 182 miles in a year. That is a lot of progress! Imagine if each mile walked got you a little further up that mountain and became a small win in your effort to build your audience and sell your books. That would be 182 wins, and that would amount to a lot of success!

Define Your Author Goals

Before you begin marketing your book, or even writing it for that matter, you should first decide what it is you want to accomplish. Setting the intention to simply sell books is fine by itself, but you may find even more opportunities await you.

Getting clear about your goals can help inform your marketing decisions. For example, if your primary goal is to use your book as a tool to sell more consulting services, it will be much easier for you to earn a return on investment from your marketing budget, because one new client might cover the cost of a year's worth of marketing. If your primary goal is to sell books, then all your energy and attention should go to activities that lead to book sales.

EXERCISE: Get Clear About Your Goals

From the list of goals below, check all that appeal to you. Next, rank the importance of your goals on the line following each item. Start with "1" as your top priority. Skip those that aren't important to you.

- ☐ Make money from book sales. _____
- ☐ Have as many people read my book as possible (little concern about profit). _____
- ☐ Win awards and accolades. _____
- ☐ Generate opportunities for speaking engagements. _____
- ☐ Establish authority in my field/become an influencer. _____
- ☐ Attract more consulting/coaching/other clients. _____
- ☐ Sell my products and services. _____
- ☐ Build my platform for other long-term goals. _____
- ☐ Be a "best-selling" author. _____
- ☐ Make a difference in the lives of readers. _____
- ☐ Contribute to a charitable cause. _____
- ☐ Have my book made into a movie/TV program. _____
- ☐ Become a full-time writer. _____
- ☐ Build a business around my book. _____
- ☐ Sell books in bulk to companies, associations, schools, retailers, etc. _____
- ☐ Attract corporate sponsorship opportunities. _____
- ☐ Become a book publisher. _____
- ☐ Other: _____. _____
- ☐ Other: _____. _____

EXERCISE: Understand Your Motivations

Answer the following questions:

What do I ultimately want to accomplish? (Think about your biggest, wildest, most exciting dream, even if it seems beyond your reach.)

_____

_____

_____

_____

What opportunities can I create with my book? (List your ideas here.)

_____

_____

_____

_____

How can I stretch out of my comfort zone (e.g., force myself to write blogs, learn to be a speaker, record videos)?

_____

_____

_____

_____

What do I need to learn to be successful? What skills do I need to develop?

_____

_____

_____

_____

Who are some people I admire and can emulate on my way to achieving my goals?

_____

_____

_____

_____

How much time can I commit each week to pursuing my goals?

_____

_____

_____

_____

What life changes do I need to make to reach my goals? (You may need to make time by watching less TV, getting up earlier, staying up later, etc.)

_____

_____

_____

_____

What will my life look like when I reach my goals?

_____

_____

_____

_____

Understand Costs and Establish a Budget

Publishing and marketing a book will require an investment in time and money. While you can bootstrap your project if you're on a tight budget, setting aside funds for marketing can make your journey easier.

While there are exceptions to every rule, following are typical price ranges for a variety of business and marketing services.

Publishing Attorney

If you have concerns about sensitive subjects, fair use rights, potential defamation issues when writing about people (in your memoir, for example), or other tricky legal questions, you may want to consult with a publishing attorney. When in doubt, it's always best to err on the side of caution when it comes to legal concerns in publishing. Experienced publishing attorneys can vet an entire manuscript for you or be hired by the hour to offer advice and consult.

Typical cost for publishing attorney: $200+ per hour, $5,000+ per manuscript review.

Business License

If you're establishing your own publishing company, it is wise to apply for a business license in the county where you live, along with a Doing Business As (DBA), which allows you to choose a business name and then open a business banking account. Like it or not, publishing a book makes you an entrepreneur. The good news is you can potentially write off many of your business expenses at tax time. Be sure to talk to a qualified tax planner or accountant.

Typical cost for business license registration: $100 to $300, depending on the county where you live.

Bookkeeper, Tax Planner, or Accountant

When you establish your business, it is wise to seek professional advice to ensure you comply with all IRS regulations. You will need a bookkeeping process, whether you do it yourself using software like QuickBooks or FreshBooks or hire it out. You will also need to keep your business and personal finances separate and file business taxes each year. When you hire contractors, you are required to file a 1099 form with the IRS each year for each contractor—a complex process that is best handled by a tax planner or accountant.

You may also need to acquire a resale license to collect and report sales tax when you sell books locally. And you may want to examine whether your business should be a sole proprietorship, LLC, or S corporation. An experienced accountant can help answer many of these questions and more, so an initial consult can be a wise investment.

Typical costs for outsourced bookkeeping: $100+ per month.
Typical fee for accountant services: $100 to $300+ per hour.
Annual fee for LLC or corporation filing: $500+.
Fee for business tax preparation and filing: $200 to $1,000+ per year, depending on business complexity.

Book Coaching

A book coach can help you get your book across the finish line by keeping you accountable. Many writers find it helpful to hire a coach to support them through the process.

Typical fee for book coaching: $2,000 to $5,000 per project.

Publishing Assistant/Virtual Assistant

Virtual assistants are freelancers who work from home and offer a variety of administrative support functions to authors, publishers, and business owners. Some are trained in book publishing and marketing processes and can take some of the burden off of you. I firmly believe every author should retain the services of an experienced virtual assistant for at least five hours a month in order to keep your marketing wheels turning. By the way, we maintain a list of virtual assistants for authors here: nonfictionauthorsassociation.com/virtual-assistants-for-authors-hire-an-authors-assistant/.

Typical fee for virtual assistant: $25 to $75 per hour and often done on a retainer basis of five+ hours per month.

Publicity Firm

Major media exposure is a goal for many authors, and an experienced book publicity firm can help reach those goals. These services do come with a hefty price tag and the cost isn't typically earned back in book sales. But if building your media resume is important to you and you have the budget, hiring a publicity firm can be a rewarding experience.

Typical fee for publicity services: $2,500 to $4,000 per month retainer, often for a minimum of three to six months.

Website Design

There are all kinds of website designers available who can create simple or complex sites. WordPress is the most common option and has the potential to grow with you as your business expands. To save on WordPress site development, ask your web developer about using pre-made templates.

Typical rates for website design: $1,000 to $3,500
An inexpensive do-it-yourself (DIY) option is available at Wix.com.

Graphic Design

There are inexpensive freelance directories like Fiverr.com which can be useful for simple projects like having social media headers designed. Just be careful when hiring freelancers for professional-level work like book covers and publishing services. You have little control over the unauthorized sharing of your work in other countries, potential copyright infringement, and other headaches that come from hiring inexpensive overseas labor. It is recommended to invest in experienced designers and publishing industry professionals when possible.

Typical rates for professional graphic design: $30 to $75 per hour.

Amazon Ads

Amazon's pay-per-click advertising platform allows you to bid on keyword phrases. Your book can then appear in all kinds of search results, but you don't pay anything until someone clicks on your ad. You can also set a daily budget of as little as $1, and once that is exhausted, your ads will stop for the day. I personally recommend a minimum budget of $10 per day in order to give your ads a chance to perform. When tuned properly, paid advertising should pay for itself in revenue generated.

Typical rate per click: $0.20 to $2.50, depending on competition.

Copywriter

A professional copywriter can help you craft a sizzling book jacket description, create detailed copy for your website, and assist with other sales copy needs.

Typical rate for copywriting: $50 to $200 per hour.

EXERCISE: Estimate Expenses

Check each of the services you expect you'll need, and then estimate the cost.

- ☐ Website design $_____
- ☐ Social media support services $_____
- ☐ Virtual author's assistant $_____
- ☐ Marketing or publicity consultant $_____
- ☐ Marketing or publicity firm $_____
- ☐ Email management tool and setup $_____
- ☐ Help with setting up online ads $_____
- ☐ Printing and mailing review copies $_____
- ☐ Copywriting expert $_____
- ☐ Graphic design services $_____
- ☐ Marketing collateral (postcards, bookmarks) $_____
- ☐ Publishing expenses $_____
- ☐ KDP, Facebook, Google, or other ads $_____
- ☐ Postage and mailing supplies $_____
- ☐ Bookkeeping and tax planning services $_____
- ☐ Business license, LLC fees, etc. $_____
- ☐ Legal expenses $_____
- ☐ Other: $_____
- ☐ Other: $_____

Costs for the above can range considerably, though once you establish a budget, you can then determine how you will allocate your resources.

What marketing budget can you set? $_____

Make Hiring Decisions

If you plan to enlist the services of a publicity firm or marketing agency, begin interviewing well in advance of your book release. Reputable agencies will want to assist in preparing for your launch and will help determine the timeline and related tasks.

Before you hire any freelancer, determine what tasks you need help with.

- ☐ Assist with self-publishing process
- ☐ Set up social media
- ☐ Manage social media
- ☐ Set up an electronic newsletter
- ☐ Manage e-newsletter
- ☐ Manage website content/updates
- ☐ Research media opportunities
- ☐ Research podcasts
- ☐ Research reviewers
- ☐ Research speaking opportunities
- ☐ Send media pitches
- ☐ Send review requests
- ☐ Send speaker pitches
- ☐ Read and responding to email
- ☐ Handle customer service inquiries
- ☐ Handle shipping
- ☐ Process orders
- ☐ Manage bookkeeping
- ☐ Moderate a forum
- ☐ Assist with marketing strategy
- ☐ Write sales and website copy
- ☐ Handle travel arrangements
- ☐ Answer phone calls
- ☐ Return phone calls
- ☐ Design website
- ☐ Edit video
- ☐ Edit podcast
- ☐ Handle customer service tasks
- ☐ Other _____

For help with locating talented virtual assistants, visit our list here: AuthorAssistantDirectory.com.

For other contractors, visit our list of resources here: NonfictionAuthorsAssociation.com/recommended-resources.

You can also use Upwork.com for locating all kinds of experienced freelancers.

PART 2

Prepare Your Website and Simplify Social Media

Discover the Power of a Mastermind Group

A mastermind group is typically comprised of three to ten people who meet regularly and support each other's goals. My own mastermind group meets once a month by Zoom and includes five business owners. Each person gets twenty minutes to share an idea or challenge and brainstorm with fellow members. I've been part of groups like this for over a decade and find them incredibly valuable for so many reasons.

If you want to take your author business to the next level, I highly recommend rounding up a few people who share your goals and values. Set a recurring meeting time each month or every other week. These groups can be helpful for accountability, inspiration, finding solutions, and so much more. Several members of the Nonfiction Authors Association have started their own groups with people they've met through our private Facebook group!

CHAPTER 5

Understand Website Strategy, Domains, and Hosting

When developing a website to promote your book, you may think you have just two choices: to launch a site for the book (*booktitle.com*) or a site for you as the author (*authorname.com*). But there is also a third option: develop a magazine-style site (see definition below). Each of these options comes with its own pros and cons to consider.

Choose a Website Style

Book Site

Designing a site dedicated to your book can have its advantages. If this is the only book you will ever write in your lifetime or the first in a series that will all be tied together and ultimately featured on the same site, then a book site may make sense. But if you plan to write more books in the future, get out on the speaking circuit, or sell other products and services, a book site may not quite suit your goals, as you will eventually be faced with managing multiple sites—and working to drive traffic to each of them. This is an important point. Website traffic is not easy to come by. If you are working to build a career around your book, you will want to drive traffic to one primary location. Make sure to consider your long-term goals.

Author Site

If your goal is to brand yourself as an influencer in your field, a professional speaker, or a media interview source, an author site can help you develop your personal brand, with your book being an extension of that brand. Having an author site creates a level of professionalism that lends itself to growing your career as an author.

While this may be ideal for authors who want to focus on branding themselves personally, keep in mind that if you plan to build products and services around your book, this may not be the ideal hub for your promotion efforts and goals. Keep reading.

Magazine Site

A magazine-style site features content that delivers value for visitors. The subject matter may be based on topics from your book or have a broader focus. Why a site about holistic cat care when the focus is hamsters? They don't really seem related at all. Fill it with news and related content on subjects related to hamster training, hamster wellness, adopting a hamster, etc.

If your book is a memoir about your experience dealing with diabetes, you might create a site focused on tips for managing diabetes, implementing a low-carb diet, living a healthy lifestyle, etc. You could also create a forum where visitors could share their own experiences with diabetes or share a link to a Facebook group you run that discusses related topics.

The ultimate goal here is to build a content-rich hub *around* your specific area of expertise and go beyond the standard five-page website. Statistically, the more content you add to your site, the more traffic it will receive, so building a site with a focus on content can have tremendous advantages. Content can include blog posts, podcast recordings, videos, interviews with peers, product recommendations, and more.

Driving traffic and engaging your audience with content marketing strategies is one of my favorite ways to attract book buyers. You will know your site visitors are interested in your topic, and once you dazzle them with the content you've cultivated, they will be even more interested in purchasing your book.

This can also be a powerful first step in forming your community. Give your potential readers a place to not only learn, but to connect with others who share their interests. Your magazine site might include a discussion forum. At the very least, your blog can include comments where visitors can share and connect.

Of course, you can add content to your book site or author site, but it may not have the same impact. Would you rather read Annie Author's personal site with her blog posts on weight loss, or would you be more drawn to a site called HealthyWeightLossNow.com?

Consider how the founder of HealthyWeightLossNow.com is immediately perceived as an industry influencer simply for building such a useful tool. This is why I believe a content-themed magazine-style site is often the best choice for nonfiction authors. It allows you to form a brand around your book(s), while at the same time attracting website visitors with valuable content *and* building your community of loyal fans.

And yes, hosting a content hub requires generating content, which absolutely means more effort on your part. But the rewards can be worthwhile, and you don't have to create all the content yourself. You can invite others to become contributors.

Real-World Examples of Magazine-Style Sites

This is not a new concept; magazine sites have been the foundation of the internet for decades now.

- CatBehaviorAssociates.com – Author Pam Johnson-Bennett runs this site, which features an excellent tagline: "America's Favorite Cat Expert." Here you will find all kinds of advice on caring for cats including behavior issues, dental health, nutrition, and more.
- DearDivorceCoach.com – Cherie Morris is an attorney, divorce mediator, divorce coach, and one of the authors of the book *Should I Stay or Should I Go?* Her site offers video tips and blog posts to help men and women navigate the divorce process.
- DrAxe.com – The tagline for this site is "Food is medicine," and it is the brand-builder for its creator, Dr. Josh Axe, a certified doctor of natural medicine, chiropractor, and author. The site is loaded with articles covering natural remedies for all kinds of medical conditions, plus recipes, food reviews, and fitness advice. While this is a magazine-style site, it is branded with the author's domain name, which is not easy to accomplish, but can be done if you produce a LOT of content.
- SixFigurePetSittingAcademy.com – Author Kristin Morrison's site offers free advice for starting a pet-sitting business through blog posts and videos. Of course, you can also enroll in her programs or buy her books here too.
- HuffPost.com – Started by Arianna Huffington as a political opinion site, HuffPo is the ultimate example of a magazine-style site. It has expanded its coverage to all kinds of topics, enlisted thousands of writers, and grown to generate massive readership. The site was ultimately sold to AOL in 2011 for a reported $315 million. Yowza!

Do You Need Multiple Sites?

Don't panic, but in addition to a magazine-style site, it might make sense to also have an author site where you can attract media interviews and speaking engagements. Many nonfiction authors host both a magazine-style site and author site because each have their own unique value. I do this myself at StephanieChandler.com.

If a magazine-style site sounds like too much work, then it's often best to stick with an author site and build from there. I stand by my recommendation to avoid creating a stand-alone book site, unless that's the only book you plan to write in your lifetime.

Obtain Domain Names

It is essential that you register your own website domain name so that you can direct your audience to your own real estate on the internet. Your site should not be part of a bigger network, like Blogger. com or something similar. There is nothing inherently wrong with free blog networks; however, when you are building a business around your book your site identity should be as professional as possible and that begins with owning your own domain.

Domain names can be purchased from many sources and domain registration is inexpensive, averaging around $10 to $15 per year. I use and recommend GoDaddy.com for domain registration.

When choosing the domain name for your website, it's best to stick with the standard ".com" extension. While new extensions are being introduced every day, most people are in the habit of typing in ".com." If you choose ".net" or ".biz" and you have a competitor with the ".com" site extension, you will undoubtedly lose site visitors to them.

Also, as much as possible avoid putting dashes, numbers, or erroneous words in your domain name. It may be harder to find shorter domain names these days, but it is worth the effort to try and find a descriptive name that isn't too long and is also memorable. You can try many word combinations until you find something that works for you. Choosing a domain name is something that requires consideration and patience and shouldn't be rushed.

You may also want to register additional domain names for marketing purposes. This includes variations on your site name. For example, my friend Karl has a site focused on healthy living to create success at RelaxFocusSucceed.com. He also registered the domain Relaxfocus*and*succeed.com, which redirects to his main site, in case a potential user types it in incorrectly.

Domain names can also be forwarded. For example, you could register the domain name for your book title (myawesomebook.com) and share that link as part of your book launch campaign, but have the domain forwarded to a book page on your magazine-style site or your author site. Domain forwards are easy to set up from your domain host and do not cost anything beyond the standard domain registration fee, which should run less than $20 per year.

Get Reliable Website Hosting

A website host manages the server where your website resides, and you will pay a monthly or annual fee for hosting. Both GoDaddy and Network Solutions also sell website hosting, email hosting, and even website templates. You can host your sites with either of these companies, or another host like SiteGround (my personal choice for hosting provider), Bluehost, or any number of available website-hosting services.

Where your site is hosted is not a huge consideration when you're starting out since most hosting services operate and cost about the same. But as your site grows and traffic increases, you will want to be sure you're hosted by a company that offers excellent technical support, data backups, and redundancy. (If the server goes down, another server takes over immediately.)

A high-traffic site can experience all kinds of problems, from bored hackers with nothing better to do than ruin your day, to server overload due to a big promotion or major media coverage driving massive amounts of traffic to your site. (What a great problem to have, right?) As your site traffic increases, you may eventually need to move to a private server. This is done through your website host and costs more than simply hosting a single site, but it is essential when your site is busy and growing.

This is something you probably will not need to do until your site has been online for a while, but it is important to understand your options for the future of your author business. For most new authors, a standard website hosting plan that costs less than $200 per year works just fine.

Understand Website Design Options

The topic of website design is a tricky one because there are so many ways you can go. I recommend WordPress as your website platform. It is robust in features and currently the most popular website platform available.

It is also important to note that Google penalizes websites that aren't designed to be mobile-optimized, which means the site adjusts to the size of the device being used. It is imperative that your site design be optimized for mobile. If your current site was designed three or more years ago, there's a good chance it does not meet current standards.

The best way to avoid many headaches when it comes to building a website is to hire a professional website designer. Prices can range, yet they don't have to break the bank. Look for sites you like and find out who did the design work. Ask friends for referrals. You can locate talented web designers from around the globe through Upwork.com, a database of freelancers. We also maintain a list of website pros here: nonfictionauthorsassociation.com/recommended-resources.

To save on web design costs, you can purchase a pre-designed WordPress template and install it yourself, if you're an adventurous do-it-yourselfer, or hire an experienced web developer to customize it to meet your needs. These themes can run $10 to $100 and can help you get your site up and running quickly. Some template sites to consider are ElegantThemes.com, ThemeForest.net, and TemplateMonster.com. When choosing a theme, be sure it is one that is updated frequently. Web technology goes out of date quickly. You should only buy a theme that is supported by the developer on an ongoing basis.

If you're on a tight budget and want a quick and easy do-it-yourself solution, Wix.com offers user-friendly templates. These are not based on WordPress, so as your site grows over the years, you will likely need a more robust solution. But it's a decent starting point.

Plan Your Website Pages and Attract Traffic

Whether you have decided to create an author site, book site, or magazine-style site, there are several pages you'll need to include on your site, and some additional elements to consider.

Home – Feature your most important content here, such as the release of your latest book and incentive to sign up for your email list.

About the Author – This should include an interesting bio about you and your qualifications for writing your book(s). Spice it up with some fun photos. Keep it fresh and interesting.

Book – Your book deserves its own page complete with a synopsis, book cover image, reader testimonials, editorial reviews, and awards received. You will also need a way for visitors to purchase the print (paperback or hardcover), e-book, and audiobook formats of the book by providing links to one or more online bookstores. If you plan to ship books yourself, you will need an e-commerce solution. PayPal and Square allow you to create simple shopping cart buttons for your website. If you want a more feature-rich shopping cart solution, compare offerings from WooCommerce, Shopify, E-Junkie, Infusionsoft, or Kartra.

Also, consider offering a sample chapter and table of contents in PDF format. You know how the cookie store at the mall offers free samples of their newest tasty treat? Or how Costco has food samplers stationed throughout the store? A free taste leads to purchases. The same goes for sample chapters of your book.

Media – A media page is where you can showcase media coverage you have received. Be sure to list all media outlets, including print, radio, and television. Also make it easy for media to cover you for a story. Include short and extended bios, plus high-resolution, professional photos that can be downloaded by media pros. You can also include sample interview questions and a list of topics you're available to speak about.

Speaker – If you speak about topics related to your book—or if you want to break into speaking—create a speaker page. List your topics with compelling titles, along with a description of what is covered in each presentation. Include testimonials from past engagements and a list of any audiences that you have spoken to. It is also a good idea to include a printable single-page speaker sheet that can be downloaded in PDF format.

Contact – Your contact page should provide a way for visitors to email you directly. Never include your actual email address, since spammers can scan your site and easily copy it. Instead, spell it out (author at mywebsite dot com), or better yet simply include a link (click here to email).

Web contact forms are fine, but I recommend also including an email link since many visitors prefer that. Be sure to include a phone number and physical mailing address, but never use your home address. Treat your book like a business and invest in a mailbox from The UPS Store or your local post office. If you work with a publicist or assistant, you can also include their contact information here.

Blog – I strongly recommend adding a blog to your site. You can share topics related to your book, quick tips, short stories, excerpts from the book, recipes, and anything else your target audience will enjoy. Update your blog at least once each week, though more often is better. Statistically, the more often you update your blog, the more traffic your site will receive. Over time your blog will bring more traffic to your site. It can be the heart of your social media strategy as well as your content marketing strategy. Blog content isn't just for written posts. It can also include videos or episodes from your own podcast.

Feature important content – Some elements should be visible across your entire website. Include links to your social media profiles and a sign-up box for your email list. I like a "locked" navigation menu, which means that as you scroll down a web page, the menu at the top follows you. This prevents visitors from having to scroll back up and makes it easy for them to browse your site.

Photos and video – If you have photos or videos to share, showcase them on your website. They can be featured on dedicated pages, within the existing pages on your site, or in your blog. Google loves sites that feature video and other media, so this can only assist in helping your site generate more traffic.

Pro Tip: If you aren't already monitoring website traffic, you should set up Google Analytics, a free tool that provides all kinds of data about your site traffic. It provides the number of unique visitors, popular keywords used to find your site, average time spent on the site, and much more. Once you set up your free Google Analytics account, you will be given a small piece of code to embed on your website. WordPress users can use a simple Google Analytics plug-in, which makes it easy to quickly add the tracking code to your site. Sign up at <u>analytics.Google.com</u>.

This should be a priority addition to your site since you can't know if your efforts are working if you're not tracking traffic results.

EXERCISE: Complete Your Website Tasks Checklist

There are several steps you will need to take to ensure your website is ready for your book launch.

Website Tasks

- ☐ Home page that is mobile-optimized. Google now penalizes sites that are not mobile-friendly. I use and recommend WordPress as a website platform.
- ☐ Book sales page with links to purchase your book on Amazon and other booksellers.
- ☐ Purchase link on your book sales page for those who wish to order an autographed copy directly from you (optional). You can use a simple PayPal merchant button or utilize another ecommerce solution, such as E-Junkie (e-junkie.com).
- ☐ About the Author page with several bios in varying lengths and professional photo(s).
- ☐ Media page, if you're working on building a portfolio of media appearances. Include your bio, one or more professional photos, your contact information, and a list of any previous media coverage you've received. (Or start building that list now.) A media page makes it easy for reporters, editors, and producers to learn about you and gather information. Plus, having one on your site will make you look like a pro.
- ☐ If you're interested in speaking, add a speaker page to your site with a list of topics you cover, testimonials from previous engagements, and video clips (if available).
- ☐ Reader discussion guide (optional) that site visitors can download after registering for your mailing list.
- ☐ Email sign-up box to your site, from Constant Contact or Mailchimp, along with incentive for signing up (bonus report, sample chapters, recording, etc.).

- ☐ Blog with articles added at least weekly. This is one of the best ways to drive traffic to your site, and your articles can be used as the heart of your social media strategy.
- ☐ Links to social media accounts.
- ☐ Contact information page that includes a mailing address (post office box) so visitors know where you're located, and an email address. A web contact form is fine, but other contact methods should be included, too. You can also acquire an inexpensive phone number from Google Voice: voice.google.com.
- ☐ A page for partners where they can easily access pre-written content to help promote your book.
- ☐ A list of services you offer, if applicable, such as consulting or coaching.

Utilize a Partners Page

Since you will be reaching out to ask your beta readers, friends, peers, and others to help promote your book launch, you can make it much easier for all to help by creating a private/hidden page on your site where they can access all the details.

When I launch a book or host any kind of promotion, I like to create a Partners page. This is a page where peers, influencers, beta readers, and others in my launch team can quickly grab information that makes it easy for them to promote the book.

A Partners page is a page on your site that isn't found in any navigation menu. It's a hidden page, so only those with the link are likely to find it. If you want extra security, you can password-protect the page, though I've never found that necessary.

I recommend creating a Partners page with details from the following checklist.

EXERCISE: Create a Partners Page

- ☐ Book sales copy/jacket copy
- ☐ Book cover image
- ☐ Author bio
- ☐ Important endorsements/testimonials
- ☐ Link to book page on your site
- ☐ Link to buy book on Amazon
- ☐ Link to book on Goodreads
- ☐ Pre-written tweets
- ☐ Pre-written social media announcements (one paragraph or less)
- ☐ List of excerpts available for publishing on partners' blogs, along with a note granting them permission to publish
- ☐ Social media memes promoting the book
- ☐ Other promotional graphics or fliers

Optimize Your Site for Traffic

Google utilizes proprietary algorithms to determine in what order websites are displayed in search results, and there are steps you can take to improve the chances of your site showing up in searches. The goal is to show up in the top ten results for keyword phrases related to your book and any related business offerings. By utilizing the following tactics, you should be able to improve your website ranking over time (and results can happen faster than you might expect!).

Improve Bounce Rate

If you want your site to be taken seriously, it should be professionally designed, formatted for easy reading, visually appealing, and easy to navigate. These factors all affect how much time visitors spend on your site, and Google takes note of your "bounce rate." The bounce rate is based on the number of site visitors who visit one page only and then leave your site without navigating to other pages within your site. Ideally, you want a bounce rate of forty percent or less. Anything above fifty-five percent is considered higher than average and indicates that your site is not engaging visitors.

Additionally, the time visitors spend on your site is a factor for Google. Do users stop by for twenty seconds and leave? Or do they navigate around and stay awhile? A general goal for time on site is about two to three minutes. Anything less could indicate a problem.

To improve bounce rates and average time on-site, look at your site objectively and compare it with others in your field. When in doubt, ask some professional contacts to give you constructive feedback. Often, a site redesign can increase traffic and readership dramatically.

Use a Responsive Design

In early 2016, Google announced that it would favor websites that are responsive/mobile-friendly. That means that when you visit a site on a tablet or mobile device, the site automatically adjusts to the screen size. Not sure if your site is mobile-friendly? Google will let you test it at google.com/webmasters/tools/mobile-friendly/. If it is not responsive, you should have a new site designed as soon as possible.

Conduct Keyword Research

When determining your keywords, start by making a list of phrases you think your potential readers and site visitors would use to find you. You can also take that effort a step further by conducting research. The free Ubersuggest tool by Neil Patel is a personal favorite for keyword research: app.neilpatel.com/en/ubersuggest/.

Add Keywords to All Pages

Every page on your website should be optimized for the search engines by incorporating a single keyword phrase on each page. The keyword phrase tells Google what that page is about and aids in helping Google direct traffic to your site. Google looks for *keyword concentration* to understand what a page is about, so it's essential that you assign a single phrase for each and every web page.

For example, if you're a professional speaker who covers internet security, your keyword phrase for your speaker page could be *Keynote Speaker Internet Security*.

Once you identify a keyword phrase for a page, incorporate it into the following:

- Page title
- Page link/URL
- The header text on the page
- Within the body of the text on the page, repeated two or three times
- Tags/keyword data

Optimize Images

Each page on your site should have at least one image, which can be a royalty-free photo from a site like 123rf.com or istockphoto.com. Images not only add visual appeal, but they can assist in optimizing your web pages. Here's how:

- Before uploading the image to your site, rename the image based on the keyword phrase for that page (example: *keynote-speaker-internet-security.jpg*).
- When you add an image to a web page, add the keyword phrase for the page to the image's "Alternative Text" field and image title. You can also add it to a caption. This assists in building your overall keyword concentration for the page.

Add More Web Pages

Once you understand how keywords work, it can be beneficial to add additional website pages to take advantage of utilizing as many important keyword phrases as possible. Using the example above, a speaker could create additional pages for each topic covered. For example, you could create a page for each of the following key phrases:

- Keynote Speaker Internet Security
- Keynote Speaker Information Technology Trends
- Keynote Speaker Data Protection

Generate Inbound Links

One of the factors Google considers when determining how your website will rank is based on how many websites feature links to your site—these are called inbound links. Inbound links tell Google that your site is popular. One way to start adding inbound links is by updating any online profiles that you have with professional associations you belong to, or other public profiles, such as your user account on Amazon, Goodreads, etc.

Write Guest Blog Posts

For inbound links, Google gives higher priority to sites with more authority, like education, government, and media sites. Therefore, another powerful way to generate inbound links is by writing guest blog posts for popular media sites like HuffPost (formerly Huffington Post) or for your favorite university. Also contribute to blogs and media sites that reach your target audience, such as independent magazines and trade association blogs. Alumni associations are also an easy target, especially if they have an ".edu" extension.

Incorporate Outbound Links

Just as Google wants to see inbound links from other sites pointing to your website, you also get some extra credit for having links on your site that lead to other sites. One simple way to do this is by including relevant links in any content that you generate. For example, if you write a blog post on your site that references a current news article, include a link to that article in your post.

Add a Resources Directory

Another way to add outbound links is by creating a page on your site specifically for recommending products and services that you like and incorporating relevant links into each recommendation. As a bonus, you could also include affiliate links and earn income from some of those recommendations. Another benefit here is that you could potentially swap links with some of the people you recommend. Let them know about your page and ask if they can reciprocate. Recommended resources benefit you as the site host and your visitors who find value there.

Generate Internal Links

Help Google "crawl" through your site by incorporating links within your content to other content on your site. For example, on a page that talks about services you offer, you could reference one or more past blog posts you've written or your resources directory. Internal links help visitors stay longer, which can also improve your bounce rate.

Utilize Video

Sites with multimedia also rank higher with Google, so adding video can be beneficial. You can record YouTube videos and embed them on your site. These can be short, "talking head" videos where you give some sort of lecture or instruction. You could also record yourself giving a live presentation or you can use software like Camtasia to record webinars or computer demonstrations. Not only can video boost your site's ranking with Google, it can also help your site get discovered when users search Google for related topics because YouTube videos often appear in Google search results.

Create an XML Sitemap

A sitemap is a tool that tells Google about the structure of your website and where to find your content so it can be properly indexed. You should submit an XML sitemap to Google, especially if you have a large site with a lot of content. One easy way to accomplish this is with a free sitemap plugin for WordPress: wordpress.org/plugins/xml-sitemaps/.

Implement a Blog

While you can optimize the heck out of your site, one of the biggest factors that Google considers is how often you add new content to your site. The easiest and most effective way to add content to your site is by blogging. Each new post gives Google another reason to locate and display your site in search results. Studies show that the more often you update your blog, the more traffic your site will receive.

EXERCISE: Complete the Website Optimization Checklist

Use the following checklist based on lessons from this chapter to ensure your site is well-optimized to generate traffic.

- ☐ Evaluate site design for professionalism and ease of use and ask others to provide objective feedback. Is it time for a redesign?
- ☐ Confirm your site is responsive and adjusts itself to fit the screen of any mobile device.
- ☐ Conduct keyword research to identify essential phrases your audience would use to find your site.
- ☐ Choose a keyword phrase for each page of your site and incorporate it into the content of the page. Repeat two to three times.
- ☐ Review images on your site and optimize them by renaming them to match the keyword phrase for each web page.

- ☐ Add more website pages based on additional topics your audience may be interested or on services you want to offer.
- ☐ Look for opportunities to add inbound links from other websites pointing to your site. What professional profiles can you update? What social media bios need to be updated?
- ☐ Consider contributing guest blog posts. What blogs, websites, or other publications reach your target audience? Are there trade associations or groups that feature newsletters or blogs where you can contribute?
- ☐ Add a resources directory to your site. Invite peers, clients, or others to contribute valued resources of interest to your target audience.
- ☐ If you're comfortable with video, create some and embed into your site pages.
- ☐ Generate an XML sitemap to submit to Google or ask your web designer to assist.
- ☐ Commit to blogging—one of the best ways to attract website traffic.

PART 2

Did You Know?

The Nonfiction Book Marketing and Launch Plan workbook was created as a companion for our popular Book Marketing Master Course.

This six-week course is delivered live once each year and is also available in self-study format. There is an optional certification program for publishing industry professionals.

Do you want support in implementing the lessons here and developing your book marketing plans? Join us for this powerful course.

nonfictionauthorsassociation.com/book-marketing-master-course-and-certification/

CHAPTER 6

Build Your Email List

When people give you their email address, they are giving you permission to market to them. This can be incredibly powerful when it comes to promoting books, events, products, and services. I firmly believe that a solid email list is one of the most important marketing tools an author can have.

While email marketing is powerful because it can convert subscribers into buyers, it is also more challenging than it used to be. We don't want to give up our email addresses because we've all been burned before. You know the drill; you sign up for a free video or report and then suddenly find yourself getting obnoxious daily "buy this" emails. Don't be *that guy*. Instead, give people incentive to sign up for your list and then deliver tremendous value so you keep them as subscribers.

You will need to sign up with Constant Contact, MailChimp, or another email service provider. It's essential to use a commercial email service for several reasons:

- If you try to send dozens of emails via Gmail, Yahoo, or other email providers, your message will likely get blocked either by your outgoing mail server or by the recipients' incoming mail server because it will look like spam. Commercial email services send emails one at a time to help ensure deliverability.
- A commercial email service gives users a piece of code you can use to put a sign-up box on your site, making it easy for users to sign up.
- You need to follow guidelines from the CAN SPAM Compliance Act, which the FTC oversees, as well as GDPR compliance guidelines for data collection from users in Europe. If you have a burning desire to read long, boring documents, look these terms up on Google and make sure you have a strong pot of coffee nearby to keep you awake! The bottom line is that a reputable commercial email service will help ensure you comply with government regulations.

Not everyone engages with social media with the same frequency. Some may check in several times a day, while others check in several times a year. So, it's likely that only a tiny percentage of your followers there are truly engaged. (There are always exceptions, of course.)

But guess what most of us do several times every single day? We check our email! And if you deliver content that delivers value to your subscribers, you can expect twenty percent or more (industry average) of your subscribers to tune in when you send an email.

Bottom Line: If building your email list hasn't been a top priority for you, it should be!

The best way to build your email list is by offering incentive to subscribe. A box on your site that says, "Sign up for my newsletter" is absolutely not enough. We are protective of our email addresses because we don't want our in-boxes overloaded. If you want to grow your subscriber base, you must deliver value.

Develop Lead Magnets

What is a Lead Magnet?

A lead magnet is incentive for signing up for a mailing list, and that incentive needs to matter to a potential subscriber. It needs to improve a subscriber's life in some way.

Your lead magnets should accomplish several of the following:

- Solve a problem for your audience.
- Demonstrate your expertise.
- Entice readers to buy your book.
- Provide entertainment.
- Deliver value.
- Dazzle readers so they want to learn more about you, your book, or your products and services.

How Many Lead Magnets Do You Need?

I recommend trying several different lead magnets to find out what works best for your audience. You can test by offering them on your website and through your social media networks. Most successful marketers create a variety of lead magnets, offering new ones on a regular basis to make sure website visitors and social media followers are inspired to sign up.

And by the way, a top goal should be to inspire your social media followers to sign up for your email list. This will ensure you can maintain your connection with them no matter what. Plus, email gives you a more effective way to reach them on a consistent basis.

Following are a wide variety of lead magnet ideas to help you build an effective strategy to grow your list so you can sell more books and build a successful author business.

List of 100 Lead Magnet Ideas to Grow Your Email List

Written Content

1. Sample chapters from your book
2. Ebook or mini Ebook
3. Beta reader sign-up
4. Report
5. Mini workbook
6. Workbook pages
7. Step-by-step instructions or process
8. Article on a hot topic
9. Bundle of articles

Audio and Video

10. Audiobook or mini audiobook
11. Video lecture
12. Real-world tutorials on how to do something
13. Animated video
14. Demonstration video
15. Funny video
16. Audio recording
17. Bundle of podcast episodes
18. Bundle of best videos
19. List of recommended videos
20. Royalty-free music

Training and Coaching

21. Training session or course
22. First module of training session/course
23. Wait list for course, event, etc.
24. Transcript from an event
25. Presentation slide deck
26. Free coaching/consulting appointment
27. Access to group coaching

Pre-formatted Templates

28. Cheat sheets
29. Scripts
30. Planning worksheets (ex: meal planner)
31. Document templates (ex: letter that can be revised and repurposed)
32. Spreadsheets with formulas built in
33. Pre-designed PowerPoint slides (or Google or Prezi)
34. Flyers for repurposing (ex: flyers to promote a band that can be revised)
35. Sales forms and letters
36. Checklists
37. Bundle of templates or digital downloads

Fun Stuff

38. Coloring pages
39. Puzzles or games
40. Recipes
41. Contest entry (research rules before hosting contests)
42. Contribute to contest (ex: sign up to donate a prize)
43. Challenge (ex: 7-day photography challenge)
44. Prompts (ex: 30 days of journaling prompts)
45. Children's book
46. Activities for kids
47. Activities for adults
48. Patterns (ex: knitting pattern for socks)

Visual

49. Infographic
50. Printable art/wall hanging
51. Printable quotes
52. Illustrated guide (ex: top restaurant guide for city)
53. Map (ex: walking trails in your city)
54. Royalty-free images
55. Tracking chart (ex: habit tracker)

Deals

56. Free trial
57. Coupon
58. Register for early access to book, course, event, etc.

59. Early bird or exclusive discount
60. Coupons to gift to friends
61. BOGO offer (buy one, get one)

Interactive

62. Quiz
63. Survey
64. Game
65. Assessment
66. Calculator (ex: estimate your weight loss results)
67. App or software access or trial
68. Invitation to private group
69. Access to online networking event
70. Speed dating or networking event

Lists

71. Helpful resources
72. Music playlist
73. Recommendations
74. Favorite quotes
75. Reading lists (ex: favorite memoirs)
76. Top 10 (or 20 or 50 or 100!)
77. Examples (ex: best birdhouse ideas)
78. Round-up (ex: links to favorite cookie recipes)
79. Spreadsheet or database (ex: list of dairy-free desserts)

Events

80. Webinar registration
81. Webinar replay or recording
82. Ticket to event (free)
83. Register for Facebook Live event (or other social media platform)
84. Get notified about event
85. Q&A with you on Zoom or other platform
86. Online concert
87. Online shopping event
88. Live training course (ex: learn how to paint birdhouses)
89. Live stream event or activity
90. Book launch party access
91. Collaborative event (several people promote event together to generate more sign-ups)

Exclusive Invitations

92. Invitation to private Pinterest board
93. Private social media group access
94. Private videos on Vimeo
95. Mastermind group access
96. Book club
97. Discussion group
98. Support group
99. Local group (ex: hiking club)
100. First 10 to respond get free access to…

EXERCISE: Plan Your Lead Magnets

What lead magnet ideas can you create? Brainstorm a list of ideas based on the challenges, interests, and pain points of your readers that you identified in chapter 3. Then pick one idea and get to work!

_____

_____

_____

_____

_____

_____

_____

_____

_____

_____

_____

_____

_____

_____

_____

_____

_____

Offer Bonus Content in Your Book

When your books are sold through retailers, you will not receive any contact information about those who buy your books. This means you can't connect or follow up with them unless they happen to reach out to you. This is one of the many reasons why adding bonus content to your book is such a powerful strategy. Providing bonus downloads to readers lets them feel they're getting extra value, while helping you build your email list and stay in touch with readers.

As you write your manuscript, or while adding the finishing touches to your work, consider what kinds of bonus content you can offer readers. Your bonus content might include a combination of the following:

- Checklists
- Worksheets
- Lists of resources
- Quizzes
- Audio or video recordings
- Templates
- Charts and diagrams
- Recipes
- Step-by-step instructions
- Maps
- Illustrations
- Printable content from your book

For example, if you have authored a book on how to get fit at any age, your bonuses might include a handful of items from the following list:

- Daily habit-tracking worksheet
- Printable lists of recommended foods or activities
- A printable chart detailing your process in easy-to-follow steps
- Bonus recipes
- A list of your favorite healthy products
- A recorded meditation
- A free sample video from your course (that leads to a soft upsell into your paid training program!)

Where to Place Bonus Links

I recommend offering three to five bonus downloads. Anything less may not be enticing enough to register, and anything more may feel overwhelming to readers. This strategy works best when you sprinkle bonus items throughout the book. Then, if the first bonus doesn't inspire a reader to go online and download it, the next one(s) might be a better fit. They only need to get excited about one of your downloads to act.

There are several places where you can mention your bonus content to readers:

- Directly in your text while discussing a related topic.
- In areas where the text has a logical break, like the end of a section or chapter.
- On blank pages, which will happen after your book is typeset. When chapters start on the right, a handful of blank pages are inevitably created in a book. And while it's fine to leave these blank, why not take advantage of this valuable real estate? Provide your typesetter with a list of "Blank Page Fillers" and have your bonus links sprinkled throughout.

EXERCISE: Identify Bonus Content

What bonus items can you offer readers? Do you already have reports or other digital downloads ready to go? If not, what could you create that readers would enjoy? Brainstorm a list and then choose at least three items.

_____

_____

_____

_____

_____

_____

_____

_____

_____

_____

_____

Capture Reader Contact Information

Next, you will need to set up a reader registration page. (Or ask your webmaster to do this for you.) Keep it simple and ask readers to register only with a name and email address, then immediately grant access to your bonus content. This should be integrated with your commercial email system, such as Constant Contact or MailChimp.

Your registration page might have a link as simple as this: MyWebsite.com/BookBonus.

Keep the link short and simple so it is easy for readers to remember and type. Also, this link should be hidden from the main navigation on your website so that only readers can locate the page. You could password-protect the page for added security, though this may not be necessary. Visitors will only get access to your bonus content if they register with name and address, so your content is protected unless they register. Adding a password could frustrate readers and create a barrier to registering.

Ultimately, adding bonus content creates a win-win situation. Readers feel like they receive added value, while you capture their email addresses and build an ongoing relationship with them. This strategy can be incredibly powerful and is recommended for anyone who writes prescriptive nonfiction and wants to build rapport with readers.

Try These Additional Ideas

As you sprinkle bonus links throughout your book, you could also use any of the following suggestions:

- Add a callout box that says something like the following: "The best way to thank an author is to post a review online. If you are enjoying this book, your review on Amazon would be greatly appreciated."
- Invite readers to a social media group that you manage. If you have a free group on Facebook, LinkedIn, or another platform, share the link and invite readers to participate. Don't have a group? Perhaps you should create one!
- Do all the above without sounding like you're selling. If your manuscript constantly references your other programs and services, you risk turning off readers. This can be reflected in reader reviews. Your best bet is to dazzle readers with your best content, both in your manuscript and in your bonus items. When you impress readers by over-delivering value, they will naturally want to know more about the other products and services you offer.
- At the end of your manuscript after your author bio, add a sales page with details about other products and services you offer, along with a call to action that inspires readers to learn more. Including this at the very end of the book will capture a satisfied reader's attention and lead him or her to take the next steps you suggest.

Example Bonus Link and ACTUAL BONUS!

Reminder: You can download pre-formatted worksheets from this book
and additional bonus content.

http://workbookbonus.com

Did You Know?

The Nonfiction Writers Conference is a multi-day event held entirely online each year. Since 2010, we have hosted hundreds of speakers including Cheryl Strayed, Julia Cameron, Anna Quindlen, Gretchen Rubin, Don Miguel Ruiz, Martha Beck, Seth Godin, Guy Kawasaki, Cheryl Richardson, and many others.

Our events feature a LIVE Pitch-the-Agents session, complimentary one-on-one consultations with industry professionals, Q&A with speakers, virtual networking with fellow attendees, bonus downloads, and much more.

Join us for our next event!

NonfictionWritersConference.com

CHAPTER 7

Choose Your Social Media Path

Though I'm a fan of social media and how we can use it to cultivate a community and reach more people, I think we've been oversold on the idea that we need to have our hands in all the cookie jars. The pressure to engage in social media has left many authors feeling frustrated by the lack of results and overwhelmed by what to do next.

Here's some good news: you don't have to tackle ALL the social media networks. Simply pick one or two—the ones where your target audience spends the most time—and leverage those well. Currently, the top networks are:

- **Instagram** – Targeting a younger audience with visual content.
- **Facebook** – A broad audience reach that can require some investment in advertising. One exception: Facebook groups are free and an effective way to build a tribe.
- **LinkedIn** – Ideal for business-related topics and connections.
- **X (formerly known as Twitter)** – A broad audience that uses the platform like a search engine to find content.
- **Pinterest** – Primarily women interested in recipes, home decorating, arts and crafts, wedding planning, fashion, and shopping.
- **TikTok** – Allows users to share short video clips. Attracts a younger audience, though interest has been shifting so this may change.

Know Your Audience

Just as with your book readers and your website visitors, it's important to understand where your audience spends time on social media and what will motivate them to connect.

- Social media marketing is not about you or your book; it is always about your audience.
- Who do you want to reach and how can you serve them? For example, if you have written a memoir about your career as a high school teacher, fellow teachers would be an ideal focus.
- What does your audience care about? What do they want to learn? What are their challenges and needs?
- Bottom line: know your audience and how you are going to engage them by providing value.

Use These Content Creation Guidelines

Content is king in the world of social media—you need something to talk about, while also providing value for your audience. As mentioned previously, your blog should be the heart of your strategy. It gives you something to share on social media and *drives traffic to your site. Following are some additional tips.*

- Use captivating headlines for blog content and social media posts. In today's world of short attention spans, people scan content and make ultra-quick decisions about what to click for more information.
- Consider how magazines attract readers. Sizzling titles can make all the difference in luring in an audience of readers. Magazines feature titles like these:
  o 10 ways to overcome insomnia,
  o 12 reasons to eat more fiber,
  o How to empty your inbox in 15 minutes or less.

  Titles matter!

- Leverage content from other sources. If you are an expert on food allergies, share articles related to food allergies. If you are an advocate for holistic ways to conquer breast cancer, share all related articles you can find. Yes, even posts from your competitors. *Especially* posts from your competitors! Isn't it better to build alliances and support each other by cross-promoting? My personal philosophy is that there is plenty of business to go around.
- Share memes, which are images that feature an inspiring quote or a brief excerpt from a book. Memes are some of the most popular content found in social media land. Create yours with a tool like canva.com.
- Share statistics and facts with eye-catching infographics.
- Share links to any media coverage you receive.
- Announce awards you win or honors you receive.
- Promote your online classes, coaching programs, and other offers.
- Engage your audience in the process of developing your new books. Ask them to vote on prospective titles and book covers.
- Ask questions and engage your community.
- Conduct polls or surveys and then share the results.
- Share each new blog post, plus additional content, across all your social networks, if you participate in more than one.

Craft Your Strategy by Platform

Facebook

Start by creating a business page focused on branding you as an author.

- Aim to share content at least once per day.
- Invest in advertising since Facebook has become a pay-to-play model. Unfortunately, their algorithms allow less than five percent of your audience to see your posts in their newsfeed. To get engagement here, you will likely have to advertise.
- Sponsor posts for as little as $5 or $10 to reach more of your audience. Be sure posts have a solid call to action, like an event or book launch.
- Promote blog posts to drive traffic and keep engagement up, provided you can afford to do so.
- Decide if this is where you should spend your time. Not all authors find that their audience is on Facebook. For example, some technical authors find it hard to engage there. Start with a small advertising budget to see if you can generate enough interest to make Facebook worthwhile.

X - Formerly Known as Twitter

X can be ideal for many authors. In 280 characters or fewer, usually enough space for a blog title, link, and a few hashtags, you can build an audience here. You can opt to become a premium subscriber and share up to 10,000 characters.

- Drive traffic to your site when you share links to content because many people treat X like a search engine.
- Repeat your posts (formerly known as tweets). For each new blog post that you share, use a scheduling tool like Hootsuite to post eight to ten times over ninety days. Example: share a new post at 9:00 a.m. on Tuesday, at 3:00 p.m. on Friday, at 11:30 a.m. the following Wednesday, and then on staggered days and times every other week for the next ninety days. We aren't all looking at X at the same time, so repeating your posts allows you to reach more people.
- Aim to post at least four times per day.
- Share posts from others that your audience will enjoy. This includes news sources and fellow authors. Remember, the key is to provide value for your target audience.
- Try to stick to your main topic. Veering too far off course can confuse your audience. For example, if you're an expert on playing the ukulele, avoid sharing tips on parenting.
- Respond to people and engage with them.
- Help your content get discovered with hashtags. A hashtag is essentially a keyword that users use to find content. If you have room at the end of your tweet, add hashtags. Example: *Book Giveaways as Word-of-Mouth Marketing #bookpromotion #publishing.*

LinkedIn

LinkedIn is a business-focused network and a powerful place for connecting with a professional audience. Every author should have a profile here, even if business books are not your genre.

- Connect with executives at companies where you want to be a speaker, or pitch them to buy copies of your book for their next conference.
- Fill out your profile with as much detail as possible. This helps you get discovered by the right people.
- Write a descriptive title since this shows up alongside your posts in groups and anywhere you engage on LinkedIn. Don't just say "author" or "consultant." Instead, try something like this: "Author of *Gluten-Free for Life* at mywebsite.com."
- Import your contacts. LinkedIn won't spam them. The system will show you who is already on LinkedIn and let you decide whether or not to send a connection request.
- Share updates such as your latest blog post title and link, just as you do on Facebook and X.
- Repurpose content from your blog and post it in full on LinkedIn, though wait at least thirty days after the post goes live on your site since Google doesn't like duplicate content. You will want to have the post on your site show up well before the version appears on LinkedIn.
- Use LinkedIn Advanced Search to locate company executives and other contacts you want to reach. For example, you can find the person in charge of the Give Back to Schools Program at Office Depot by searching for company name "Office Depot" and keyword "give back to schools program." Many employees of large companies share this kind of information in their LinkedIn profiles.
- Sign up for LinkedIn Pro if you want to send LinkedIn Mail to contacts outside of your network.
- Convert your LinkedIn account to a Creator account, which makes it easy for others to follow you and allows you to feature your chosen content at the top of your profile.
- Apply to be an instructor with LinkedIn Learning: https://learning.linkedin.com/instructors.

Pinterest

This network is used for sharing photos and videos. It is popular with the female demographic, especially for topics like bridal planning, home decorating, crafting, cooking, and fashion. Users create "boards" where they can save their favorite "pins" (photos or videos). Not all audiences are found here, but it doesn't hurt to try it out and see if you can reach yours.

- Give Pinterest a try if you are writing for the above niches or create any visual content (images or videos). Even if you are outside of these popular genres, you might be surprised how Pinterest can drive traffic to your site.
- Pin photos from each post on your blog, which will automatically add a link back to your site.

- Give each pinned post a keyword-rich title and description. This will help your pins get found by those searching Pinterest for your type of content.
- Have fun creating keyword-rich boards related to your audience such as "Best Tips for a Healthy Marriage" or "Holistic Solutions for Back Pain."

Instagram

There is no denying that Instragram is growing each day, although its user base skews toward those ages eighteen to thirty-five. This visual network relies on photos and videos for sharing. It's also owned by Facebook so any advertising you do on either platform can be shared on both.

- Be clear about your focus. If you're an author of a book about going green, stick to posting earth-saving content at least ninety percent of the time.
- Stand out by infusing your personality in your posts.
- Aim to post at least once per day, though more often is even better.
- Install the app on your phone so you can share easily and often.
- Use a tool like Canva to customize images with your logo or quotes.
- Share hashtags to help users find your content.
- Tag other Instagram users and businesses in your posts to build alliances and gain interest from their audiences.
- Use geotags to mark your location. For example, tag yourself at a conference you're attending. Others who are interested in the event may stumble across your content and become fans.

EXERCISE: Develop Your Social Media Strategy

If you're just getting started, pick two social media networks where you believe your audience spends time. Facebook is a good place to start for many because it's user-friendly and a huge percentage of the population visits Facebook daily. Add LinkedIn if you're focused on a business audience or Instagram if you have visual content that appeals to younger generations.

Identify your top two social media platforms.

_____

_____

_____

_____

_____

_____

Study how others are leveraging social media and pay attention to what you like and don't like. Make note of those strategies here.

_____
_____
_____
_____
_____
_____
_____
_____
_____
_____
_____
_____
_____

It's important to share content and engage with your audience each day. Brainstorm ideas for content you can cultivate and share with your audience.

_____
_____
_____
_____
_____
_____
_____
_____
_____
_____
_____
_____
_____
_____

An effective social media presence can be managed in fifteen to thirty minutes per day. Commit to blogging and using social media for at least six months. It takes time to build momentum, but when you start to see the results, you will know it's worthwhile.

Leverage Social Media Groups and Online Forums

Part of building your Tribe of Influence is knowing where your audience spends time. Chances are good that your readers are actively participating in one or more groups on Facebook, LinkedIn, or another platform.

Online groups and forums have a tremendous amount of potential, yet they can be underutilized by authors. When you connect with your audience in a community where members share common interests, the opportunities are truly endless. Let me share an example.

After my husband died unexpectedly in 2013, I spent hours searching Google for resources to help me and my son get through the most challenging time in our lives. Along the way, I joined several forums where widows discuss their journeys and support each other. I've remained an active member of three of them ever since.

Now, imagine the possibilities when I finish writing my book for fellow young-ish widows. (Someday, I promise!) I've been an active community member in these groups, reaching thousands of my target readers. Here are some ways I could leverage these groups in support of my book:

- Invite group members to contribute interviews for the book or my blog, thus building anticipation and interest in advance.
- Invite group members to be a guest on my podcast.
- Survey members of the group about their experience, letting them know it's for my book, and then share the results in the book.
- Invite group members to be beta readers.
- Ask the administrator if it's okay to hold a book giveaway for the group.
- Ask group members to connect with organizations and associations they belong to where I could speak or contribute to the blog, newsletter, or podcast.

Can you see how powerful a group can be?

To locate groups to join, search LinkedIn and Facebook for keywords related to your industry to find active groups that cover your area of interest. You can also search Google for industry keywords, plus "group" or "forum" to uncover even more resources.

And while you should join related groups, also consider starting your own. It doesn't cost a dime to host a group on Facebook or LinkedIn, yet the potential to reach thousands of people is tremendous.

EXERCISE: Leverage Online Groups

Look for groups that reach your target audience on Facebook, LinkedIn, Yahoo, and other forums. Join one or more groups and start engaging well in advance of your launch so that you aren't a total stranger when you announce your book. Then, when it's time to launch your book, you can potentially have hundreds or even thousands of ideal readers interested.

Group Name	Contact Name	Website Link

EXERCISE: Consider In-Person Groups

Trade associations, Meetup groups, alumni groups, and related groups can potentially garner helpful support for your book.

Group Name	Contact Name	Website Link

PART 3

Get Ready to Rock Your Launch

Are you enjoying this book?

One of the best ways to thank a fellow author is to post a review on Amazon! If you find this book helpful, please take a moment to post a review. Thank you!

P.S. You should include a note like this one in your books, too!

CHAPTER 8

Connect with Tribe of Influence for Endorsements and Review Copies

From the lists of tribe members, influencers, and media pros you assembled in chapter 2, you will find there are many reasons to reach out. You may ask them to contribute a blog post or request support with social media or launch efforts. Following is an example of an actual pitch letter I sent to peers who I have friendly relationships with when I launched my last book.

Connect with Your Tribe of Influence

Greetings friends,

This is going out to a small group of my closest industry friends. My new book, _The Nonfiction Book Publishing Plan: The Professional Guide to Profitable Self-Publishing_, launches on Wednesday 9/26!

Would you please help spread the word on launch day and beyond? I am happy to send you a copy—just reply with a mailing address. Or you can download a digital copy here.

I've put together a special web page with copy, pre-written tweets, images, excerpts for your blog, and other details to help get the news out.

Visit the Partners page here.

Thanks so much for your support! Please let me know how I can return the favor.

All my best,

Stephanie

This letter was friendly and personal since it was sent to people who I have relationships with. I didn't want it to be overly formal, though a more formal approach might work with peers you're not close to. If you plan to ask for various types of support, such as contributing guest blog posts, sharing on social media, and announcing your book to a group, you may start by writing the first influencer letter and then modify it to meet the needs of each request.

EXERCISE: Write Your Tribe of Influence Letters

- ☐ Include book title and brief description.
- ☐ Detail time frame for release.
- ☐ Explain clearly what you're asking for.
- ☐ Include a link to your Partners page.
- ☐ Offer a complimentary review copy of your book.
- ☐ Ask how you can support the influencer with his or her next initiative.
- ☐ Write a different letter for each type of help you're asking for.
  - o Asking friends and peers to help spread the word.
  - o Asking for bulk sales orders.
  - o Offering a complimentary review copy for consideration. (For professors, media professionals, trade associations, key contacts, etc.)
  - o Inquiring about speaking engagement opportunities.

EXERCISE: Prepare Launch Content—Checklist

There is a tremendous amount of copy needed to host a successful book launch. Don't put this off! Write your copy in advance so you're ready for launch day.

- ☐ Write three compelling descriptions of your book—short, medium, and long versions.
- ☐ Develop your book jacket copy from the descriptions you've written.
- ☐ Write two author bios—a longer one for the last page of your book and a single paragraph for your book jacket. Include a call to action such as: "Visit myawesomesite.com to download bonus content."
- ☐ Create a Partners page on your website.
- ☐ Write a pitch letter for endorsement requests.
- ☐ Write several blog posts to publish on your site during your launch campaign.
- ☐ Write several blog posts that promotion partners can publish on their sites.
- ☐ Write social media posts, including longer and shorter versions, that you can share.
- ☐ Write social media posts your partners can easily share.
- ☐ Write an announcement to share in any online groups you belong to (Facebook, LinkedIn, etc.).
- ☐ Write the email announcement you will send to your own email list.

☐ Extract several excerpts from your book that can be made available to other sites to publish and publish on your own blog. Include a brief bio at the end indicating that the article is an excerpt, along with a link to a web page to learn more about the book.

☐ Write media pitches for traditional and online outlets. (Covered in chapter 11.)

☐ Other:

☐ Other:

☐ Other:

Start Requesting Endorsements

In the months before your book is published, you can begin reaching out to authors, celebrities, and influential industry contacts to request endorsements for your book (also known as "blurbs" or testimonials). Ideally, endorsements should come from authors and key influencers in your field, and the more well-known, the better. While endorsements are not mandatory, they can add credibility to your work.

The goal is to get at least one well-known author to endorse your book so you can print the quote on your book jacket. If you successfully round up more endorsements than will fit on your book jacket, they can be listed in the opening pages of your book.

While you may think that big-name authors are unreachable, this is not always the case. Smart authors know that endorsing a book enhances their marketing efforts since they gain added visibility with your readers. And the fact is that it never hurts to ask. All they can do is say no, but they just might surprise you and say yes!

How to Send Endorsement Requests

The key to getting the attention of well-known authors is to show up like a pro. Avoid telling them your whole life story and don't appear desperate for their endorsement. Also, avoid mentioning how this is your first book, you're self-publishing, and you have no idea if anyone will ever buy your work. That will not inspire a good outcome.

Contact information for even the biggest authors is almost always available. Search their websites or reach out via social media messages. You might be surprised by who reads their own mail on all of the social media networks. Also, well-known authors may have a publicist or media contact and it's perfectly fine to reach out to those folks. If you can't locate this information on their websites or social media networks, ask their publishers for a publicity contact.

An endorsement request should be short and get to the point quickly. Here's a sample request that you can copy and send out via email:

> Hi <author name>,
>
> I am a big fan of your book <title>. <*Briefly* explain why you loved the book in two sentences or less.>

PART 3

As a fellow author, I'm reaching out to ask if you would consider providing a brief endorsement for my book. <title> will be released later this year by <publishing company name>.

<Insert a description of *one paragraph or less.*>

The synopsis, table of contents, and full manuscript are available to download here: <Link to a Dropbox folder or Bookfunnel.com link>.

I have an extensive publicity plan to support the launch so your effort won't go unnoticed. It would mean so much to me to receive a testimonial from you. Is this something you can provide?

Thank you for your consideration!

Warm wishes,

<your name>

Note that this note starts out by complimenting the author's work. This demonstrates you are a fan of his or her work and creates an instant rapport. (Flattery will get you everywhere.)

Mentioning the publishing company also adds credibility *unless you are using a common self-publishing service*. If that is the case, omit the publishing company information. The unfortunate reality is that self-publishing services like KDP will be recognizable and an author with a major press can be turned off. And if this is the case, please do yourself a big favor and establish an authoritative publishing company name. (You can learn more about how to self-publish effectively by reading *The Nonfiction Book Publishing Plan*, which I cowrote with Karl W. Palachuk.)

Write two or three of the most compelling sentences you can craft about your book and why readers will enjoy it. Then, share a link to access the synopsis, table of contents, and the full manuscript (if available) or at least two sample chapters. This removes all potential barriers and delays, making it easy for the endorser to say yes.

The sad reality is that most people will not read an entire manuscript prior to endorsing a book. They may skim it over to be sure the author is capable, but most will not have the time or inclination to read your work. Don't take it personally; we're all busy. If you had to rely on a big-name author carving out eight hours to read your entire manuscript, you would likely never acquire an endorsement.

What Happens After You Reach Out

When reaching out by email or social media, it is typical to receive a response within a few days. If you are lucky, that response will include the endorsement right in the body of the message.

Some may ask you to send along sample endorsements they can consider. Yes, this is more common than you may realize. It can be an awkward task to write your own endorsements, but it's smart to have three to five written and ready to send along if requested. Big name authors will often tweak one of your options slightly and then give you permission to use it.

Don't be discouraged if an author declines to endorse your book. You could still mail him or her a review copy with a personal note later, as it could lead to future opportunities or a post-publication endorsement, which can be a big win.

The bottom line is that endorsements can enhance the credibility of a book, so do not be afraid to pursue them with gusto. Make a list of ten to twenty authors and start asking. With any luck, you will end up with so many testimonials that you'll need to add a page or two to the beginning of your book to accommodate all of them!

Consider a Foreword—Or Not

A foreword is written by someone influential in the field to introduce the book to readers. It is meant to add more credibility to the book. Asking for a foreword is a much bigger request than asking for an endorsement. A foreword typically requires that the writer first reads the entire manuscript and then crafts several insightful pages to open the book. However, you might be surprised to learn that like endorsements, some forewords are written by the author of the book or a ghostwriter, and then approved by the influential person who agreed to provide the foreword.

For most books, adding a foreword is optional. However, a foreword can enhance credibility if it comes from someone well-known. For example, if you author a self-development book but you don't have any related credentials, it can be wise to ask a therapist or physician or another relevant expert to write the foreword.

It is far easier to acquire one if you already know someone influential who is willing to write one for you (or approve one that you write). Or perhaps have someone you know make an introduction. Otherwise, you will follow a similar process with the endorsements, and you may find it more challenging to get a positive response.

EXERCISE: Complete Endorsements To-Do List

☐ Spend time searching Amazon for books in your genre and make a list of authors to contact. It's best to read their books first.

☐ Search for contact information for each author on their websites and social media networks. Well-known authors often list a publicity or media contact. You can also try sending a direct message through their social media accounts.

☐ If contact information is unavailable, reach out to the publisher to ask for a publicity contact.

☐ Attend an event where you have a chance to meet the endorser.

☐ Consider if you know anyone who could make an introduction for you.

☐ Write a compelling endorsement pitch letter.

☐ Send out your pitches prior to publication of your book.

☐ Mail a signed review copy to everyone who provides an endorsement, along with a personal thank-you note.

☐ Post-publication endorsements can be valuable, too. Don't be afraid to send out review copies, even to the authors who initially decline to endorse.

EXERCISE: Locate Book Endorsement Contacts

Identify influential authors from your genre who could potentially endorse your book. One way to do this is to search for similar books on Amazon, and then click through other recommended titles to discover authors you didn't even know about. Endorsements can also come from celebrities, industry influencers, or top professionals in your field. Whether you know them or not, you have nothing to lose by asking.

Name	Email Address

Plan Your Advance Review Copies

Publishers have been sending out advance review copies of books (also known as ARCs) for decades. ARCs were created by traditional publishers to give media outlets a chance to write reviews, which were published to coincide with the official book release. Even today, most major magazines and newspaper outlets expect ARCs to consider books for reviews.

The practice of printing ARCs has expanded to include internet media pros, bloggers, podcast hosts, social media influencers, and early readers who can post reviews on Amazon, Goodreads, and other sites. While traditional publishers often make ARCs of books available up to six months in advance of a book's release to get the attention of top media outlets, indie authors and self-publishers might only print ARCs a few months or even weeks ahead of a book release. Or you might not print them at all. It depends on your goals.

An official ARC is typically printed with a temporary cover or something denoting that it is an advance review copy and not available for resale. Bookstores are not allowed to sell ARCs and are expected to remove them from any kind of circulation.

Do You Need ARCs?

Your goals and your publishing timeline will be factors in deciding if ARCs make sense for you. If you are focused on getting major media attention and published reviews, then ARCs should be planned into your publishing timeline. Just keep in mind that book reviews in major media outlets are exceedingly difficult to get and are usually reserved for top authors from traditional publishers.

Self-published authors may have better luck with marketing to smaller trade magazines, blogs, and industry-specific magazines. (Hello, *Cat Fancy*!) I encourage you to think beyond book reviews. Some publications might feature an excerpt from your book, and interview with you, or ask you to contribute an article.

If media attention is not your primary goal, you might not need ARCs at all. You could instead send contacts from your Tribe of Influence a copy of your book just before it is published or even after.

Where to Print ARCs

<u>Lulu.com</u> offers quick and easy publishing solutions for uploading print-ready files and ordering books. You can order ARCs in small or large quantities. You can also print and bound an ARC at your local copy shop, though it won't look quite as professional as a bound copy.

Develop Your Strategy for Review Copies

Beyond advanced review copies, you should absolutely plan to send out copies of your book post-publication. Sending out books can lead to a variety of opportunities:

- Acquiring reviews on Amazon and beyond.
- Attracting media coverage, podcast interviews, etc.
- Building word of mouth.
- Gaining exposure with influencers through blogs, social media, etc.
- Enticing a new prospective client to work with you.
- Getting your book considered for bulk purchases.
- Being invited or hired as a speaker.

I know I've said this several times already, but it's important to be crystal clear about your target audience, who should receive a copy of your book, and why you're sending it to each person. I cannot emphasize this enough.

Many authors and publicists send me all kinds of books. I've received novels, relationship guides, business books, and even poetry books. While I appreciate the gesture, it is often a wasted effort because I don't review books. While I wish I could review and recommend every single book, there will never be enough hours in a day to do so. The only exception is when I receive publishing industry books. I do look at those and sometimes receiving a review copy leads me to invite the author to be a podcast guest. Know your audience!

Where to Send Review Copies

It is important to identify who should receive copies of your book based on how they may be able to impact your book promotion efforts. Following are some suggestions.

Anyone mentioned in the book – If, within your book, you reference someone as an example, a case study, or recommend him or her for any reason, you should send a copy. It's flattering to be mentioned in a book, and many people who are honored this way will want to tell others about the book.

Endorsers – Anyone who provides a prepublication endorsement or foreword should receive a signed copy from you, along with a note of thanks.

Beta readers – People you give early access to your manuscript prior to publication are known as beta readers. In this case, you will typically share a digital copy of your book with the goals of receiving early editorial feedback, plus reviews posted online once the book is released. (More on beta readers coming up.)

Amazon reviewers – Look at competing books in your genre on Amazon and locate the reviews section for each one. You can click on each reviewer to see his or her public profile on Amazon. Some include an email address or website link so that you can contact them. Many reviewers are thrilled to receive a complimentary review copy.

Bloggers – Search for bloggers in your genre who review books, publish author interviews or book excerpts, or conduct book giveaways. You can reach out first to ask if the blogger would like to receive a review copy, or you can mail a copy with a personal note.

Book review bloggers – Search Google for *<genre>* + *"book review."* Also, try searching for titles of competing books plus "book review" to see where they have been reviewed.

Podcasters – I consider this one of the top opportunities for authors to gain exposure. Search podcast directories like iTunes or Stitcher to find podcasts that reach your target audience, then locate the website for each program and search for submission guidelines. Ideally, you should craft a polished pitch to be a guest on the show, and then send along a copy of the book to the host prior to your interview. You want the host to be familiar with your book so he or she will reference it during your appearance.

Social media and YouTube influencers – Locate the most influential social media stars who reach your target audience and send a copy of your book. For best results, always try to create a win-win situation. Instead of asking for promotion, what can you offer these leaders? Can you interview them for your own blog or podcast? Can you co-promote a book giveaway or contest? Top social media influencers are often inundated with requests for promotion. If you want to get their attention, you'll need to get creative and offer something that delivers value to them and/or their followers.

Media pros – Reporters who cover topics in your genre are ideal recipients of review copies. Remember, book reviews aren't the only point of media outreach. You could send a copy of your book along with a well-designed media sheet that features you as an expert and lists a variety of potential interview topics, making you a strong potential source for a future interview.

Online groups – As mentioned earlier, online groups can be powerful for connecting with your ideal readers. You could send a review copy to the group moderator and offer to host a giveaway with group members. Offering to give away three copies as a promotion to a group with thousands of members can bring a tremendous amount of exposure.

Association and nonprofit leaders – Locate groups where your target readers are members and send copies of your book to the board of directors or planning committee members. You may want to speak for these groups, contribute to their blog or newsletter, have your book featured in their online store, or even have your book given away to their new members. Associations can bring tremendous opportunities!

Prospective clients – If you're a consultant, coach, or advisor of any kind, you can use your book to impress potential clients. You can send books out as lead magnets to hard-to-reach prospects or send a copy after you've made initial contact to help close the deal. Authoring a book is a big accomplishment and can help boost your credibility with new clients.

College professors – If your book would make a great text or case study for certain college courses, research professors who teach those courses and send a copy. Having your book selected for the course can lead to ongoing sales each quarter, trimester, or semester.

Specialty retailers – Want your book considered for sale in specialty stores, gift shops, restaurants, pet stores, garden centers, or other non-bookstore retail outlets? Send a copy to the store owner or manager.

Corporations – If your book would make a useful giveaway to corporate employees or clients, send a copy to the head of the right department at any company that would be a good match for your book. For example, if your book assists with emotional well-being, pitch it to the head of human resources for a progressive company like Google or Intel.

Speaking opportunities – Whether you're seeking to get free or paid speaking engagements delivered in-person or by webinar, your book can help you stand out and capture the attention of event planners and hosts.

Your Tribe of Influence – Based on the Tribe of Influence exercise you completed in chapter 2, consider some ways your personal tribe could potentially help:

- Buy your books in bulk for the company they work for or introduce you to someone who could make a bulk purchase.
- Invite you to speak at an event, in-person or by webinar.
- Post a positive review on Amazon, Goodreads, or another online retailer.
- Announce your book via social media or an email list.
- Introduce you to media contacts.
- Connect you with a podcast interview opportunity.
- Host a contest or giveaway with a key target audience.
- Interview you for a blog or print publication.
- Connect you with a corporate sponsorship opportunity.

How Many Review Copies Do You Need?

Plan to set aside copies of your book to give away to traditional and online media pros, potential reviewers, and other influential people who can help spread the word about your book. The number of books you give away is up to you, but my philosophy is that the more eyeballs you can get on your book, the better your chances of building an audience. I recommend authors plan to distribute at least 100 copies. ***In fact, I challenge you to locate at least 100 media contacts and influencers to give copies of your book to!***

EXERCISE: Prepare Your Review Copies Contact List

Plan to send review copies of your book to people who have requested them, plus influential people, potential clients, media pros, bloggers, reviewers, and anyone to whom you want to offer an early copy of your manuscript or a complimentary copy of your book. You may have already identified some of these people during the Tribe of Influence exercise in chapter 2.

Reminder: You can download a preformatted spreadsheet with the following worksheets here: http://workbookbonus.com.

Name	Email Address

PART 3

EXERCISE: Build Anticipation for Your Book Launch

Starting as far in advance as possible, build anticipation and buzz for your book launch.

- ☐ Put your book cover on your website with a big "coming soon" announcement.
- ☐ Build your mailing list. Make sure you have an email sign-up box on your website and add it to your Facebook page as well. Don't have an email list yet? Consider ConstantContact. com, mailchimp.com, or aweber.com.
- ☐ Get your social media accounts set up if you don't have them already. You don't need to do it all, but you should pick at least two of the top networks: Facebook, LinkedIn, Pinterest, X, or Instagram. Start sharing news about your book months in advance.
- ☐ Have social media headers created with your book cover image and a "coming soon" announcement.
- ☐ Have memes (graphics that have quotes over images) created for social media. Use these to brand quotes from your book or to simply brand your website link at the bottom of each image. You can purchase images from sites like 123rf.com or iStockphoto.com.

CHAPTER 9

Enlist Beta Readers

Beta readers are people who get early access to read your book for free. Yes, I said free. The primary objective is to get people talking about your book as soon as it's launched. At the same time, you can build a base of raving fans who also write reviews. Beta readers can be organized in a private Facebook group and given special privileges, such as access to a course you offer to thank them for their efforts. They should also be asked to post book reviews on Amazon, Goodreads, and other sites, and be encouraged to help you spread the word about the book. Some authors like to solicit editorial feedback from beta readers, too.

You don't necessarily have to ask beta readers for editorial feedback unless that's something you personally want to do. In his book *On Writing: A Memoir of the Craft*, Stephen King said he only allows a few trusted friends to read his manuscripts in advance. You can run into some frustration when you have too many cooks in the kitchen, so the decision is up to you.

However, beta readers can play an essential role in your book launch by helping to create reviews and spread the word via social media. So, whether or not you want feedback on your manuscript, giving early access to the book before it's released can have many benefits.

Decide How Many Beta Readers You Need

My personal feeling is that you should have as many beta readers as you can find. Our goal as writers should always be to get our books in the hands of as many people as possible. And yes, that means giving it to them for free. If each reader tells just a few friends about the book, you can earn that "lost sale" back over and over again.

Worried that your manuscript will get shared with people outside of your beta reader community? During the 2017 Nonfiction Writers Conference, Seth Godin addressed this common fear. His response: *"Your problem is not piracy. Your problem is obscurity."* Godin encouraged readers to give their books away freely because the more eyeballs you can get on your book, the bigger your fan base can grow.

Romance novelists use a formula of giving away the first book in a series or selling it at a super low price to get readers hooked on their series. While you may not write a series of books, if you sell related products and services, giving copies of your book away can be useful. You can attract readers to your mailing list, social media networks, and get them interested in your related products and services.

The bottom line: enlist the number of beta readers that feels right to you. Maybe you just want twenty or so because this strategy makes you a little uneasy. That's your prerogative. However, I encourage you to think bigger and consider how much more substantial your book launch can be when you have 100 or more people posting reviews and announcing its release to their own audiences.

Learn How to Work with Beta Readers

One of the best ways to organize early readers is to invite them to a private Facebook or LinkedIn group where you can connect with them and get them involved in your book launch process. Ideally, you should position participation in your beta reader group as a special opportunity for people who enjoy your genre and get to read your new book before the general public does.

Since not everyone visits online forums regularly and some may miss your posts there, be sure to add your beta reader group to a private email list. Once you've added readers to the group, engage with them and show them how to help you. If you're seeking feedback on the manuscript, give them a reasonable deadline to respond. Two to four weeks should be enough.

Also give them guidance about the kind of feedback you're seeking. Do you want them looking for punctuation, spelling, and grammatical issues? Do you want them to track changes in Word and send back a red-lined copy? Or do you want them to type up some general feedback? Setting expectations at the beginning can prevent your readers from going rogue and giving you feedback you don't want.

Speaking of feedback, provide a list of questions you want them to answer. Here are some examples:

- Is there enough level of detail throughout the book or are there areas that need clarification? If so, which areas?
- Were there enough real-world examples or are there areas where additional examples would be helpful?
- Does the content flow in a logical order? If not, how could it be improved?
- What is your overall opinion of the book? What would make it better?

The questions shown above could also be incorporated into a document where participants answer these questions for each chapter, if that's the level of feedback you want. Ideally, readers would fill out their answers and return the document to you. You can also create a Dropbox folder where you can share revised versions of the manuscript and where your readers can submit their responses or red-lined copies of the manuscript.

You will need to guide your readers in how to participate in the promotion process. Make it as easy as possible for them to get involved. Here are some suggestions:

- Make them aware of the book's release date.

- Ask them to share via social media and their own email lists.
- Provide them pre-written tweets, memes, book cover images, and content for easy sharing (a private page on your website with details can work just fine).
- Ask them to post reviews on Amazon, BarnesandNoble.com, Goodreads, and more.
- Offer to provide guest posts for their blog.

Remember to keep communicating with your beta readers and help them feel involved in your book launch. Let them know the status, thank them for their reviews and shares, and make sure they feel appreciated.

EXERCISE: Create a Beta Reader Application Form

Create a sign-up form for those interested in joining your group. You can use free Google Forms to accomplish this, or a tool like SurveyMonkey. You should ask a few questions to screen participants. Here are some examples:

- What is your favorite <genre> book? (You want to make sure you're enlisting readers who actually enjoy reading books in your genre.)
- Why are you interested in being a beta reader?
- Are you interested in providing feedback on the manuscript?
- Are you willing to help promote the book to your own network upon its release?
- Are you willing to post one or more reviews of the book? Where will you post them?
- How else will you assist in spreading the word about the book upon its release?

You could also have applicants give links to their own social media profiles and websites, if this is criteria you care about. I don't think that having a substantial platform should be the only reason to enlist beta readers, and it could significantly limit participation, but it can be useful to know how wide a reader's reach may be.

Locate Beta Readers

Here are some ways to find your beta readers:

- Your own social media networks and email list.
- Ask your colleagues, family, and friends to participate.
- Ask your colleagues, family, and friends to reach out and invite people in their networks.
- Online groups that reach your target audience. For example, if you're writing a memoir on your battle with breast cancer, locate groups for people who are navigating the same illness.
- Reach out to trade associations, alumni groups, and other professional organizations that reach your target audience, and ask them to help you get the word out to their members.

- Post to writers' forums and communities:
  - o absolutewrite.com/forums/
  - o mywriterscircle.com/
  - o Goodreads has a public group specifically for finding beta readers: goodreads.com/group/show/50920-beta-reader-group

Sample Beta Reader Pitch Letter

Here is the actual letter I sent out to our email list during my last book launch.

Dear friends,

I am thrilled to announce my new book coming this fall, co-authored with my friend Karl Palachuk: *The Nonfiction Book Publishing Plan*.

Calling All Beta Readers

We are looking to build our launch team, which means we are making the manuscript available for early reading to our tribe of beta readers.

What's a beta reader, you ask?

Beta readers are part of an author's launch team. They get early access to a book in exchange for agreeing to help spread word-of-mouth, write reviews, and share feedback.

Our book has already been through lots of editing, so we're not necessarily looking for that kind of feedback (unless you notice something glaring that we need to know about). But we are seeking your overall opinion of the book, as well as support in sharing the news when the book launches in late September.

No special qualifications are needed to be part of the beta reader team! All you need is a willingness to support the book launch and an interest in reading the manuscript (which will be sent to you digitally in PDF format).

To thank you for your participation, you will receive the following:

- **First access to the manuscript.** Besides our editors, absolutely nobody has seen it yet—not even friends or family.
- **An invitation to our private Facebook discussion group**, created exclusively for our launch team.
- **Access to our marketing plans** so you can not only follow along, but you can learn from us as we go.

- **Immediate access to the bonus downloads included with the book**: list of Resources for Writers—over 200 links!, List of Book Printers, List of Book Distributors, Report: *How to Utilize Amazon Ads*, Report: *Essential Book Marketing Tactics for Nonfiction Authors* (28 pages!), Book Marketing Action Plan Template (Excel spreadsheet), Cash Flow Forecast Template (Excel spreadsheet), Book Pricing Calculator (Excel spreadsheet).
- **Other cool surprises.** We have a few ideas in the works so you can expect some extra love coming your way.

If this sounds like fun to you, then please fill out the quick application form and we'll be in touch within a few days. Deadline to apply: August 17.

APPLY TO BE A BETA READER HERE

Want to learn more about the book or get notified when it's released?

VIEW BOOK DETAILS HERE

Thanks for all of your support!

Stephanie

You can use my letter above as a template for your own letter.

Sample Social Media Post

Beta readers wanted! My book is coming out soon and I'm seeking beta readers to provide editorial feedback, post reviews, and help support the launch. If you're a fan of <genre>, I'd love for you to join our team. Apply here: <link>

Manage Your Beta Reader Program

- Consider using a tool like BookFunnel.com to distribute your manuscript to beta readers. This allows you to make the digital version of your book available in the reader's preferred format, such as Kindle, Nook, or iPad reader. You can also simply share the manuscript in a Dropbox folder. Make sure it includes a copyright statement like this: *Copyright © 2024 by Stephanie Chandler*. (Hint: Add parentheses around the letter "C" and Word will automatically create a copyright symbol: ©.)
- Use a collaborative tool such as betabooks.co or betareader.io when seeking editorial feedback.
- Engage with your beta readers often to keep them interested and make them feel like they are a valued part of the process.

- Acknowledge your beta readers somehow. You could thank them in a page printed in your book or in a blog post on your website.
- Take it a step further and offer extra incentive for their participation, such as membership in a program you manage or extra downloadable content, if you feel this is necessary. Added incentives never hurt!
- Show your gratitude by thanking them several times throughout the process. Let them how they've impacted the book and what it means to you.

EXERCISE: Use This Beta Readers Action Checklist

- ☐ Set a goal for how many beta readers you'd like to have: _____.
- ☐ Create an application form for prospective beta readers.
- ☐ Put out a call for beta readers through your email list, social media, and other sources you've identified.
- ☐ Set up a private Facebook group (or LinkedIn or other community group where your readers spend time).
- ☐ Create an email list for your beta readers so you can easily communicate.
- ☐ If you want to receive feedback on your manuscript, develop guidelines for beta readers to follow.
- ☐ Determine how you will make your manuscript available to your beta readers. You could save a PDF version to a free Dropbox location, or use a tool such as Book Funnel to manage distribution of your files. Betabooks.co or betareader.io are other options to help manage the editorial feedback process.
- ☐ Engage beta readers by informing them of the process along the way. Let them know the status of publishing, the planned release date, and other details that allow them to feel like part of the process.
- ☐ Remember to show your gratitude to beta readers.
- ☐ You will also engage them in your book launch. Keep reading to learn how.

Reminder: Download Bonus Items

You can download and print many of the exercises and checklists featured in this workbook along with additional bonus content here: http://workbookbonus.com.

PART 4

Navigate Traditional and Online Media Like a Pro

Did you know?

The Nonfiction Authors Association is a vibrant community for writers to connect, exchange ideas, and learn how to write, publish, promote, and profit with nonfiction books. With a mission to help authors make a difference in the world, NFAA is the leading resource for nonfiction writers who want to learn how to navigate the publishing industry and reach your goals.

Membership benefits include:

- **Exclusive Author Advisor email sent every Friday** with **curated media leads** and featured **templates, checklists, recordings, and reports** from our massive members-only content archives to make your author journey easier.
- **Author Brainstorm Exchange and Member Round Table,** monthly group meetings held online with Zoom. Members and industry pros share ideas, challenges, and solutions.
- **Featured listing on NonfictionBookClub.com** for added visibility with readers.
- Popular members-only **Facebook group** to connect with authors and industry pros.
- **Meet-the-Members program** where you can share your book announcement with our email list, blog, and social media community.
- **Discounts** off our **year-round Nonfiction Book Awards program**, author toolkits, and other items in our author store.
- **Discounts of our exclusive courses,** including the Book Publishing Master Course and Book Marketing Master Course, both with **optional professional certification**.
- **Discounts off the** Nonfiction Writers Conference, held entirely online since 2010.
- **Discounts** with **NFAA partners** including Lulu, Office Depot, Findaway Voices, and more.

Ready to reach your author goals? Join us!

NonfictionAuthorsAssociation.com/join

CHAPTER 10

Leverage Media Opportunities

Open any newspaper or magazine and notice how each article includes quotes and advice from experts. Often, these quotes come from authors. Tune in to any talk radio show, the *Today Show*, or even your local news programs, and authors are constantly in the spotlight. Did you know media professionals from print, radio, and television frequently search Amazon.com for authors of books related to their planned subject matter?

Understand How Media Impacts Book Sales

There is a reason why the word "authority" begins with "author." Having a book published makes you an instant *author*ity on your subject matter, and thus, a logical source for media interviews.

Publicity Sells Books—Sometimes

Landing a media interview is always exciting, no matter where you are in your author journey. An interview for a podcast, blog, newspaper, magazine, or television show can lead to substantial book sales. And sometimes it doesn't.

Several years ago, I received a call from *Wired* magazine. The reporter interviewed me as part of an upcoming cover story and I was ecstatic. When my copy arrived in the mail a few months later, I found my interview highlighted in a sidebar next to the main cover story (about digital marketing). It was fantastic placement, captured my advice well, and I was sure it would lead to TONS of book sales.

But it didn't. Sales reports showed a bump of a few dozen copies, but nothing to get excited about.

What I suspect happened is that my sidebar interview was overshadowed by the main story. Readers likely glanced at the sidebar and then breezed past it since there were larger parts of the story to digest. It was a big lesson learned; not all media coverage leads to book sales.

I met an author at a conference several years ago who shared a similar story with me. She had appeared on *Oprah*. Yes, *Oprah*—a dream of many writers. She flew from San Francisco to Chicago, shared her advice during a brief segment, and her book sales fell flat.

When she dissected what happened, she realized that her book was mentioned in the ribbon at the bottom of the screen under her name, but Oprah didn't talk about the book. Oprah didn't hold up the book or sing its praises like she was known to do with other books. The author's book was only mentioned in passing on the screen and book sales were dismal.

When Does Publicity Lead to Book Sales?

You can never be sure if an appearance will lead to sales, but there is always that possibility. I've been surprised by the results of some of the media interviews I've done. Once, a sponsor hired me to do a media tour on behalf of their product. With the help of an expensive media tour company, I gave over twenty interviews on radio and television on an early morning in a Sacramento-area hotel suite. It was grueling and led to very few book sales. But it did lead to lots of website traffic and sales for the sponsor, which was the primary goal and the reason I was hired.

I've also done interviews on traditional radio where I've had to be up at 3:00 a.m. on the West Coast in order to speak with a radio host in New York covering the morning commute shift. My book was mentioned, and it sold a few dozen copies. Considering traditional radio has thousands of listeners, the return wasn't too impressive.

Comparing those results with several podcast interviews I did around the same time, the podcast programs were significantly smaller than the traditional radio shows, yet I sold more books.

The big difference was that the podcasts reached *my ideal audience*. They may have had smaller listenership, but when the host recommended my book, the loyal listeners made purchases. That was when I fell in love with podcasts to generate publicity.

I've also had brief mentions in major newspapers and smaller blogs and magazines that have led to impressive book sales. And I've had just as many mentions in publications that didn't generate big sales. The reality is that you can never know for sure if a media interview will lead to sales.

Why Bother with Publicity?

Every appearance on a program and every feature in a publication builds your resumé and increases your credibility as a subject matter expert. As your media resumé builds, so can other opportunities. Putting links to interviews on your website can impress potential readers, clients, and people who want to hire you. It can help you attract speaking engagements, corporate sponsors, and business opportunities.

You'll also become a more seasoned expert with each interview you give. You will get more comfortable with the process, you'll figure out how to better get your message across, and you'll start to feel like a pro. It's like anything that is new to you; the more you practice, the better you will inevitably get.

It's also not uncommon for one interview to lead to another. That appearance on your local morning news program can lead to invitations to be on other local shows or programs in different metro areas. An article in your local newspaper could end up syndicated to national newspapers. Or an editor from a different paper could see the article and want to interview you for another story. That podcast interview you gave could result in two or three other podcasters inviting you to be a guest on their programs. An interview in a magazine could lead to another reporter noting your expertise and contacting you months later for a quote for a similar story.

Media coverage can also help you attract a traditional publisher if that's your goal. When you can say you've appeared on dozens of programs and publications, your author platform is elevated and becomes much more interesting to decision makers.

Keep all of this in mind as you pursue media opportunities. Your mileage may vary, but each interview will likely bring benefits that you may not realize for months or even years. Be sure to celebrate every interview opportunity, whether it leads to book sales or not.

Prepare Before You Pitch

You should know that reporters, editors, and producers NEED story ideas. In other words, *they need authors as much as we need them.* When you can make their jobs easier by bringing story ideas they can run with, you both win.

Keep in mind that media outlets each have unique goals and requirements that you should know about before you begin pitching.

Newspapers – Depending on the publishing schedule, newspaper reporters need content daily or weekly, which means they are *always* on the hunt for good stories. Be sure to contact the right reporter for your topic. If your pitch is about Small Business Week, don't waste the Lifestyle reporter's time.

Another note about newspapers is that these journalists take their jobs very seriously. Never send a gift or anything that could be perceived as a bribe. It will likely end up in the trash. If you want to send a handwritten note or a copy of your book, that's fine, but avoid boxes of chocolate or other gifts.

Magazines – Magazines have a much longer lead time before going to press. They usually work three to six months ahead of schedule. If you want to pitch your book as an ideal holiday gift, you should start in June for larger publications. Smaller magazines may work just a few months ahead.

Local newspapers and magazines – It's far easier to get local coverage than national coverage. Oftentimes, the larger publications pay attention to stories from smaller publications, so you never know what opportunities can arise later. Also, your hometown newspaper may syndicate some of its content nationally. A feature in a local paper can lead to follow-up stories in other publications.

Local TV news – Provided that you can craft your pitch to fit in with the tone of your local programming, your nearby morning and evening news shows can be excellent places to build exposure and get some experience in front of a camera. Keep in mind that television is a visual medium. Producers want to bring their audiences dynamic content like cooking segments, puppy training,

PART 4

and other live demonstrations. If you can bring something visual to your appearance on a news show, make this a key feature in your pitch, since it will absolutely help you stand out.

National TV news – It's far easier to get national media coverage after you've landed local coverage. The bigger shows like *Good Morning America* and the *Today Show* want to see "clips," which are the recorded segments of you performing successfully on-air. They can't afford to take chances on inexperienced guests and need to know that you are a safe choice to serve as a guest. Once you have some clips of local appearances, include those links in pitches to national television programs.

Radio – News talk radio programs, such as NPR, can bring valuable exposure for authors. Most radio interviews are brief, lasting just five to ten minutes, unless you're invited into the studio to chat with a host for a longer period. The advantage of radio is you don't have to be local—you can call in to stations across the country. Make sure you have access to a good landline and audio equipment. (I love my Blue Yeti microphone.)

Podcasts – There are many benefits to being a guest on a podcast. First, most podcast interviews are much longer than traditional radio. While a traditional morning radio show might have you on for eight minutes, podcasts often feature guests for fifteen minutes, thirty minutes, or a full hour. This gives the audience a chance to connect with you, decide to like you, and then make a purchase.

Podcast interviews are often promoted online in the weeks leading up to the appearance, shared across social media, and then archived for listeners for all eternity. If the show reaches the right target audience for you, it could have just one thousand listeners and lead to far more book sales than a major traditional radio show. Podcast interviews can be powerful!

Blogs – While you might not have previously thought of blogs in terms of media coverage, you may want to reconsider. Many blogs serve as online publications and reach plenty of loyal readers. Think of sites like HuffPost, WebMD, and Mashable. If you're an author of a health book that gets mentioned in a feature article on WebMD.com, you can expect some book sales and other opportunities will follow.

Own Your Expertise

Before you begin pitching the media, you should get clear about your subject matter expertise. For many nonfiction authors who write prescriptive books, your expertise is clear. If you write books on small business growth, you're an expert in small business. If you write books about wellness, you're a health expert. If you write books about home decorating, you're an expert in home design.

It gets a little tricky when it comes to memoirs or other narrative nonfiction books, but you are still an expert and have value to offer. For example, if your memoir covers your experience as an adopted child, you have clear expertise in adoption. If your memoir details your journey as a caregiver for ailing family members, perhaps your expertise is in caregiving or in maintaining family communication. If you wrote a book on military history, you could share relevant facts related to Memorial Day.

The point is that you must claim expertise in something in order to position yourself as an authority in the eyes of the media.

Imposter Syndrome—the Challenge is Real

One of the most common challenges for authors is taking ownership of his or her expertise. If you're feeling like you're not THE ultimate expert, rest assured you're not alone. Many authors feel this way. However, you should also know that you don't have to be the world's foremost authority on your subject matter. You just need to have enough confidence to convey what you do know. Remember this: you know more than the average person about your subject matter. That can make you an expert.

I don't know anything about reptiles. If you write books about the care and feeding of reptiles, you are one thousand times more knowledgeable than I am. Who cares if there are other reptile experts out there? Your own experiences and opinions make you unique.

By the way, nobody has all the answers. Nobody! You aren't expected to know your industry inside and out. You should know enough to speak with authority, but the world won't stop spinning if you don't have every single answer. A media trainer would tell you to answer a question you don't know like this: "I'm not sure about that, but what I am sure of is ..." See how easy that is? Politicians do this every day!

There are lots of authors who write financial advice guides. There are lots of authors who write health books, religious books, self-help guides, and business books. The market has room for many experts in every single category.

I'd like to challenge you to claim your expertise and your unique perspective on your subject matter. Your point of view is likely different from your competitors and that's a good thing. Be different, share your knowledge, and know that you have just as much of a right to claim your expertise as your competing authors do.

EXERCISE: Claim Your Expertise

Fill in the blanks with your own information, then use this as part of your author bio.
_____ is the author of _____
and an expert in _____.

Write a Newsworthy Pitch

Before you begin reaching out to media pros, make sure you have a newsworthy pitch. A new book release rarely qualifies as newsworthy, unless you're a celebrity or you've embarrassed yourself to the core on a reality show. When you consider that hundreds of thousands of new book titles are released each year, you can see how this is rarely newsworthy. Instead, tie your pitch into a topic that is timely.

Here are the primary ways to tie-in your media pitch:

- Upcoming holiday, such as Valentine's Day, Columbus Day, or Christmas.
- Offbeat holidays like National Pi Day, National Hat Day, or International Square-Dancing Month (yes, this is really a thing!). See HolidayInsights.com or Chase's Calendar of Events (rowman.com/page/chases) for more unusual days.
- Anniversary of a significant event like the 1989 earthquake in San Francisco or the anniversary of the moon landing.
- Upcoming event with wide appeal, like the Olympics or the Grammys.
- Current trends like the rise of mental health issues in teens who have phones or the latest statistics on obesity rates.
- Current news stories that you can hook into. For example, if a major politician is caught cheating on his spouse and you're a body language expert, contact local media outlets and let them know that you can evaluate his speech and show whether or not he's being truthful.

When you can tie your story idea into something relevant that's happening in the news, you significantly improve your chances of your story getting picked up.

Use Industry Statistics and Trends

Another way to appeal to media pros is to tie-in your pitch with recent industry statistics. For example, in the past week, I saw an article AND a TV news segment on recent statistics that were released about the current state of student loan debt. One headline read: "Student Loan Debt: A $1.5 Trillion Crisis."

Talk about an effective pitch! This is a sizzling headline; it's time-based because it ties in with recent facts and it has broad audience appeal. It's a topic that could fit in with a news radio program, news television program, or newspaper. It could also work in a local magazine.

Now, consider what niche media outlets this topic could work for. It could fit into parenting, financial, business, and school-related publications, blogs, and podcasts. This is a topic with tremendous potential.

Though it helps to leverage recent statistics, they don't have to be hot off the press to pitch a story. Statistics published within the past couple of years can always be referenced and used to position a story. For example, if you want to pitch a story about screen time for teens, all you need to do is track down some relatively recent industry reports about screen time—and you may even find several reports to reference in your pitch. Provided the statistics come from a reputable organization, you can use them.

If you're really adventurous, you could compile your own statistics by conducting surveys and then share those results along with your media pitches. But this isn't necessary if you can find other relevant sources to cite.

Trends fall into this same category and can cover a lot of topics. Common trends we see reported in the news include social media use, diets, popular sports and hobbies, fashion, teen obsessions, and children's toys. Weird or unusual trends can also get coverage based on the novelty factor. (Ax throwing, anyone?)

If a media outlet reports on an increase in families adopting turtles as pets, you can reference that story in a pitch to a different media outlet. Here's an example:

> According to *Turtle Lovers Magazine*, turtle adoption rates have tripled in the last five years. As the author of *The Wonderful Lives of Turtles* and an expert on turtle breeding, I can share with your audience five surprising reasons why turtles make ideal pets.

There are lots of ways to track current trends. Google offers interesting data at <u>trends.google.com</u>. You should also follow leading publications in your industry to stay on top of the latest trends and news and create some Google Alerts to track trends in your industry as well.

Leverage Your Expertise to Get Media Attention

When you can't tie-in to a timely topic, statistic, or trend, your next best bet is to offer up your expertise, tailored to the target audience. The idea here is to give your media outlets suggestions for evergreen topics that have direct appeal with their audience. For mass market programs, your pitch needs to have broad appeal. For example, if you've authored a book about how to buy and sell a home, you might pitch your local media outlets any or all of the following:

- Proven ways to sell your home in a slow market
- Five tips to prepare your home for a hot summer sale
- Three biggest mistakes home buyers make and how to avoid them
- The ten hottest local markets to buy an affordable home
- Five signs it's time to sell your home

The above pitches have broad appeal for a local market since most viewers will buy or sell a home at some point in life. Additional examples of topics local media programs like to cover:

- Cooking demonstrations and tips
- Healthy eating tips
- Information on diet trends
- Pet care tips
- Ways to get organized
- Activities for kids
- Parenting advice
- Tips for managing school, homework, kids' sports, and other kid-related activities
- Home decorating strategies
- Money saving tips

For more ideas, watch your local news shows and take note of the stories they feature. Also, read your local newspapers and hometown magazines. What stories do they cover? How could you see yours fitting in?

EXERCISE: Brainstorm Media Pitch Topics

Brainstorm a list of potential topics you could pitch the media throughout the year. List topic ideas that you could pitch to various media outlets. What tie-in opportunities are available (holidays, news cycles, etc.)? What topics from your book have wide audience appeal?

_____
_____
_____
_____
_____
_____
_____
_____
_____
_____
_____
_____
_____
_____
_____
_____
_____
_____
_____
_____
_____
_____

CHAPTER 11

Become Your Own Publicist

Providing radio programs, podcasts, and television shows with a media sheet can help you stand out as a potential guest and make you look like a pro. In fact, you can attach your media sheet to your email pitches.

Your media sheet can be created and maintained in Word, though you should save it as a PDF before sending it along. As a general rule, PDF documents look more professional. They can also be read across all kinds of platforms including PCs, Macs, and mobile devices.

Your media sheet should include some combination of the following:

- Professional headshot of you
- Brief bio that could be read as an introduction
- List of books you've written
- Mention of past media appearances
- Your areas of expertise
- Website and social media links
- Contact information, including cell phone number
- Sample interview questions

Not every host will use your proposed interview questions, though many are grateful to receive this information because it makes their jobs easier. The host may ask you a few questions from your list, every single question on the list, or none at all. Always be prepared for curveballs.

The following is one of my own media sheets, which you can use as an example.

PART 4

Sample Media Sheet – Page 1

Stephanie Chandler is the author of several books including *The Nonfiction Book Publishing Plan: The Professional Guide to Profitable Self-Publishing* and *The Nonfiction Book Marketing Plan: Online and Offline Promotion Strategies to Build Your Audience and Sell More Books.* Stephanie is also founder and CEO of the Nonfiction Authors Association, a vibrant community for writers, and the Nonfiction Writers Conference, events conducted entirely online since 2010. A frequent speaker at business events and on the radio, she has been featured in *Entrepreneur, BusinessWeek,* and *Wired* magazines.

Stephanie Chandler is available for interviews on the following topics:

- ❖ Traditional and self-publishing (she has done both herself)
- ❖ Book marketing, online and offline
- ❖ Profit strategies for nonfiction authors
- ❖ Revenue stream development
- ❖ Corporate sponsorships for influencers
- ❖ Book launch campaigns
- ❖ Advanced book marketing strategies
- ❖ Content marketing for authors, speakers, consultants, and entrepreneurs

Websites and Social Media:

- ❖ StephanieChandler.com
- ❖ NonfictionAuthorsAssociation.com
- ❖ NonfictionWritersConference.com
- ❖ Facebook.com/AuthorStephanieChandler
- ❖ Facebook.com/NonfictionAuthorsAssociation
- ❖ Linkedin.com/in/StephanieChandler
- ❖ @NonfictionAssoc

Contact Information:

<Email>
Direct: xxx-xxx-xxxx
<Mailing address>

Sample Media Sheet – Page 2

Sample Interview Questions:

1. What are the benefits of being an author? Should all professionals consider writing a book?

2. How should someone go about writing their first book? Any tips for getting a manuscript written?

3. How do you know if your book idea is a good one?

4. Should authors be worried about people copying their ideas or stealing their content?

5. What are some of the pros and cons of traditional publishing and self-publishing?

6. Why do you think self-publishing has increased in popularity over the years?

7. Why did you choose to leave traditional publishing in favor of self-publishing?

8. What are the steps involved in self-publishing?

9. What are the steps involved in traditional publishing?

10. What are some of the biggest mistakes authors make when self-publishing their books?

11. How important is bookstore distribution?

12. Should authors also produce audiobooks, and if so, how can they do this?

13. What are some of your favorite book marketing strategies for authors?

14. For authors who don't yet have much of an audience, what are some of the top ways they can sell books?

15. How important is social media for authors?

16. Which social media networks should authors use?

17. As an author yourself, what would you do differently if you were starting today?

18. Why did you start the Nonfiction Authors Association and what are the benefits of joining?

19. Why did you start the Nonfiction Writers Conference?

20. How do you deliver a conference online?

21. What one piece of advice do you want our listeners/viewers to remember today?

PART 4

Sample Media Sheet – Page 3

Stephanie Chandler has been featured by the following media outlets:

Forbes • Entrepreneur Magazine Inc. • Wired Magazine • BusinessWeek.com • New York Times Online • Los Angeles Times Business • Sunrise 7 (Australia's version of The Today Show) • Writer's Digest • More Magazine • Sacramento Bee • Success Magazine • San Francisco Chronicle • Sacramento Business Journal • Wells Fargo Small Business • AllBusiness.com • CBS Marketwatch • Small Business Opportunities Magazine • Home Business Magazine • Prosper Magazine • California Journal • Fort Worth Business Press • Young Entrepreneur.com • Reuters • SOHO Business Journal • Sales Pro Magazine • Good Day Sacramento • Success Magazine for Women

• Minnesota Star Tribune • NPR • CNBC • ABC News 10 • Small Business Administration Radio • Capital Public Radio

Books by Stephanie Chandler:

- *The Nonfiction Book Publishing Plan: The Professional Guide to Profitable Self-Publishing* (Authority Publishing, 2018)
- *The Nonfiction Book Marketing Plan: Online and Offline Promotion Strategies to Build Your Audience and Sell More Books* (Authority Publishing, 2013)
- *Own Your Niche: Hype-Free Internet Marketing Tactics to Establish Authority in Your Field and Promote Your Service-Based Business* (Authority Publishing, 2012)
- *Booked Up! How to Write, Publish and Promote a Book to Grow Your Business* (Authority Publishing, 2010)
- *LEAP! 101 Ways to Grow Your Business* (Career Press, 2008)
- *The Author's Guide to Building an Online Platform: Leveraging the Internet to Sell More Books* (Quill Driver, 2007)
- *From Entrepreneur to Infopreneur: Make Money with Books, eBooks and Information Products* (John Wiley & Sons, 2006)
- *The Business Startup Checklist and Planning Guide* (Aventine Press, 2005)

See more details: www.StephanieChandler.com

EXERCISE: Prepare Potential Interview Questions

Make a list of potential questions you expect you would be asked during interviews.

_____

_____

_____

_____

_____

_____

_____

_____

_____

_____

EXERCISE: Create Your Own Media Sheet

Prepare for pitching media by creating a professional media sheet that you can send along with pitches. You can also post it to the media page on your website.

Craft Your Media Pitches

When sending a pitch directly to a media source, it's best to start with email and most importantly, keep it brief. Reporters, editors, and producers are busy people who receive a lot of email. They scan quickly and are used to hitting the delete key at lightning speed; so get to your point right away. Your opening sentences should cover the five Ws:

- **Who** – Describe who you are as an expert and author and why you're the best person to deliver this interview.
- **What** – This is your pitch, whether it is based on tips or a tie-in with a current event or holiday. Make sure it sizzles like a magazine headline.
- **When** – Is this pitch time-based? How soon are you available to give the interview?
- **Where** – Are you offering to do a demonstration in their studio? Are you inviting the reporter to an event?
- **Why** – Explain why this topic will appeal to their audience and how it will benefit them.

Some additional considerations when sending a pitch:

- Address the host, reporter, or producer by name, when possible.
- Provide a simple list of three to five discussion points to illustrate the story you're pitching.
- Briefly explain why the topics are relevant to the audience.
- Mention previous interview experience since it increases confidence with the host or producer and lets them know you'll be a good guest. If you don't have previous experience, skip this part.
- Assure the host that your goal is to provide an informative interview for his/her audience.
- State your credentials.
- Offer a complimentary copy of your book for review. Or mail a copy with a note tucked inside. If the host/reporter has a chance to review your book before the interview, you'll have a much better chance of it being mentioned.
- Given that so many interviews are now happening via Zoom or Skype, you can stand out by mentioning you have the right equipment to be successful.

Here's an example of a pitch:

Dear Rhonda Reporter,

Instagram is growing faster than any other social network, according to this report in *Social Media Trends* magazine. With National Small Business Week approaching (May 21-25), I'd like to propose an article on the top five ways small businesses can leverage Instagram to gain more customers. And if this topic isn't quite the right fit, here are some alternatives:

- Instagram mistakes to avoid for small business
- How to create compelling Instagram content
- Insta Stories: What they are and how to use them to sell products and services

I know you frequently cover social media trends in your column, though I don't believe you've addressed how businesses can grow with Instagram marketing. I have some unique perspectives and concrete examples to share that your audience won't find anywhere else. I'm the author of *Instagramify Your Business,* and since 2015 I have been teaching small businesses how to generate revenue with Instagram using ethical marketing practices that get results.

I have a home-based studio with professional lighting, a high-quality web camera and microphone, and high-speed internet so I'm able to conduct remote interviews professionally. Are you interested in an interview on any of these topics? Thank you very much for your consideration.

Best wishes,

Joe Author

Understand Press Releases

Press releases aren't as powerful as they once were, though there are still times when a release can be useful. As mentioned previously, the release of a new book is rarely considered newsworthy, unless the author is a celebrity. However, notifying your networks and local media about a book release doesn't hurt and could possibly lead to some opportunities.

A press release on your website can make you look like a seasoned professional, showing that you take your book seriously. If you distribute your release through online distribution services, it can potentially drive some traffic back to your website and possibly even lead to some book sales (though keep your expectations low). You can also share a link to a press release on your site when sending more informal pitches, which can impress media professionals.

How to Write a Press Release

A press release should be brief—one to two pages max—yet include enough details that a reporter could write a short article based solely on the information provided. Here are some additional guidelines:

- Read several sample press releases before writing yours so that you understand the proper format. Some good sources for locating professional releases are BusinessWire.com and PRNewswire.com.
- Start with a proper heading that includes your contact information. When listing phone numbers, indicate a day and evening number (reporters may call at odd hours) or simply list your cell phone number. You do not want to miss these calls; so make it as easy as possible to reach you.
- Give the release an enticing title that captures the reader's interest in **BOLD CAPITAL LETTERS**.
- Double-space the body of your release for easy reading.
- Include in the first paragraph the basics of who, what, where, when, and why. You should lay the foundation and include your hook immediately. Remember that you want to engage and prompt a response from the media.
- Use testimonials you have received for the book or excerpts from book reviews. As awkward as it may be, you should also quote yourself.
- Close with a brief summary of the book including publisher details, ISBN number, price, and where to purchase a copy.

Following is a press release outline, and then an example of an actual media release used by Wasabi Publicity.

PART 4

Actual Press Release Sent by a PR Firm

Nonfiction Authors Association community member, Dr. Cholet Josué, engaged Wasabi Publicity to help launch his memoir. They graciously shared their initial press release so you could see an example of how this is done by professionals.

Media Contact
<name>
Wasabi Publicity, Inc.
<phone, email address>

For Immediate Release:

Physician and Neuroscientist Shares Immigrant Story, Tools for Living a Good Life
Bahamian-born Haitian-American author Dr. Cholet Josue
offers brain tools for good living

[DATE] Over the course of his journey from Haitian immigrant to neuroscientist, Dr. Josué has discovered the three things he says we need to live a good life: financial stability, health, and a supportive community. Now, he is using behavioral cognitive neuroscience to recommend three tools people can use to access these essentials:

- Self-compassion
- Emotional intelligence
- Critical thinking

"If any human being can get these three tools into their brain," Dr. Josué says, "they can get the resources they need to live a good life. My goal is to educate people about their brains, emotions, and behaviors, because that's what governs our lives."

In his forthcoming book, *Twelve Unending Summers: Memoir of an Immigrant Child* (spring 2019), Dr. Josué shares what originally inspired his research into living one's best life: his immigrant story. The tools he used to survive and thrive have become a centerpiece of his work as a physician and neuroscientist today.

"Some of the things I did well were using critical thinking and emotional intelligence," says Dr. Josué. "And one thing I've always had—though not in a perfect way—is self-compassion. What self-compassion teaches us is not to feel sorry for ourselves. There is a balance in that—to see your flaws and your imperfections and accept them with compassion. Critical thinking, emotional intelligence, self-compassion—those are the things that carry us as human beings."

For more information, visit www.drjosue.com.

About: Dr. Cholet Kelly Josué is a Bahamian-born Haitian American author and physician seeking a home among the three cultures that have played a role in his life. Born in the Bahamas of Haitian parents who wanted their children to experience their ancestral roots, Cholet moved to Haiti with his siblings when he was four years old. There he spent the next twelve years of his life reveling in a simple and decent, if checkered, childhood until he was sent across the Caribbean Sea in a wooden boat to join his mother in South Florida after the death of his father.

While still an undocumented immigrant, Cholet earned a Bachelor of Science degree in chemistry from Florida Atlantic University. Then he spent the next six months at the University of Miami law library preparing to represent himself in the trial of his life: the quest to become a legal resident.

Cholet received his medical degree from Morehouse School of Medicine in Atlanta, Georgia, and did his residency at the University of Illinois in Chicago. Currently, Cholet practices medicine in the greater Washington, DC, area with a functional and integrative approach and draws on his special interest in behavioral neurology and neuropsychiatry. He is a member of the American Medical Association, the American Psychiatric Association, the Maryland Psychiatric Association, the American Neuropsychiatric Association, the Cognitive Neuroscience Society, and the Society for Neuroscience.

His forthcoming book (spring 2019) is entitled *Twelve Unending Summers: Memoir of an Immigrant Child*. Visit www.drjosue.com.

PART 4

Sample Press Release Outline

FOR IMMEDIATE RELEASE

Business Name
Address
Contact Person
Phone
Email

CATCHY HEADLINE INDICATED IN BOLD CAPITAL LETTERS

Date – City, State – Lead paragraph including summary of who, what, where, and when.

Body of press release should include three to six paragraphs. Include quotes from yourself or others (make sure to get their permission). Write the content as if it were an article you were reading in a magazine. Don't forget to double-space the text.

Paragraph Two

Paragraph Three

Paragraph Four

Paragraph Five

About the Author

Brief Overview of Book

How to Locate Media Contacts

There are two primary ways to locate media contacts. You can purchase media lists, which can be expensive, or do the research yourself. There are also services that offer media leads, which we'll discuss shortly.

If you have a budget, purchasing media lists can be a big time-saver.

- **Cision** offers the most comprehensive media lists available: cision.com/us/products/database.
- **Media Contacts List** is another service where you can purchase lists: mediacontactslist.com.
- **A News Tip** is an interesting database that builds media lists based on tweets and written articles. You can search for keywords and locate journalists who've tweeted or written articles about your keywords and then add them to a media list that you build. However, access to the contact information will run $200 per month: anewstip.com.
- **Buzzsumo** tracks popular content based on how often it has been shared via social media networks. You can enter keywords to find articles and the influencers who share them and then hunt down the authors, blogs, or media outlets. Full access starts at $79 per month.

Build Your Own Media Contacts List

Nearly all major media outlets have websites with easy access to contact information for reporters, editors, and producers. In fact, they make it almost ridiculously easy to find email information because they need story ideas. While this information is easy to locate, the research can take time.

The following are ways to locate media contact information:

Google – Use the search engine to search for and locate media sources. For example, if you want to reach media in your old hometown, you can search Google for "newspaper Indianapolis," "news Indianapolis," "radio Indianapolis," etc. You can also search for terms like "list of weekly newspapers." My search for that term turned up a list for Los Angeles: laalmanac.com/media/me04a.htm. It also produced a comprehensive list (minus contact information) here: xpresspress.com/weekly-newspaper-media-list.

Once you locate a media outlet, you'll need to look at the website to find contact information. Some may publish submission guidelines, list reporters who cover specific topics, or publish a complete directory of staff.

Mondo Times – This free directory lists US media outlets (primarily magazines) by topic, which can help you identify publications to target: mondotimes.com/topic/index/html. There is also a directory for international publications: mondotimes.com/2/topics/7.

Trade Pub – Provides a list of trade publications in a variety of categories. Trade publications can be an excellent target because they reach niche audiences and often welcome new content: tradepub.com.

World Newspapers – If you're looking for global publications, this will come in handy: world-newspapers.com.

Media.info – This directory lists television, radio, magazine, and newspaper media outlets in the UK, Australia, and Ireland: media.info/uk.

Be on the Lookout

Whether you're surfing social media or reading a magazine in your doctor's office lobby, keep an eye out for reporters who write about topics that relate to what you do. Most reporters have a specialty area of focus. If a reporter writes about the stock market, he/she probably won't be writing about the latest in genealogy research.

Find the reporters who can connect with your message and reach out. You can even send a quick email to compliment a story along with a note that says you're available as a source if the reporter writes a follow-up article. Reporters maintain databases of expert sources they can reach out to. You never know when an opportunity might arise down the road.

LinkedIn

You can use the advanced search feature to locate users by keywords, company name, publication name, or job title. If you're not yet connected, you'll need to either request an introduction from a mutual friend or pay to upgrade your LinkedIn account so that you can email contacts outside of your network. You can also track down a contact name, return to Google, and then search for an email address.

Access More Media Opportunities

Help a Reporter – This free service delivers daily email roundups of reporters seeking sources to interview. It's free to sign up, though the competition is fierce. To land opportunities here, read the emails as soon as they arrive and respond quickly to opportunities that match your expertise. Details here: helpareporter.com/.

Pitch Rate – Similar to Help a Reporter, you can subscribe to daily email roundups of reporters seeking expert sources for interviews: pitchrate.com/.

ProfNet – This paid service hosts a database where experts, authors, and other sources can list themselves as available for media interviews. Reporters, producers, and other media pros can access this database for free and contact you directly if you're listed here: profnet.prnewswire.com/ProfNetHome/Profnet-experts.aspx.

EXERCISE: Research Media Contacts

Media Outlet	Contact Name	Email	Phone

PART 4

EXERCISE: Prepare Your Media Pitches

☐ Write a pitch for local television programs, newspapers, magazines, and radio shows. Remember, it's often much easier to begin with local media coverage.

☐ Write a pitch for national media outlets. If you have any local media experience, share those links in your pitch.

☐ If you decide to send a press release, write that as well.

CHAPTER 12

Generate Online Publicity Opportunities

While there are a lot of rules around how to pitch traditional media sources (newspapers, television, magazines, and radio shows), the rules for pitching online sources are often looser, and the opportunities could keep you busy every day of the week. Following are some strategies you can use to get exposure for your books.

Get Interviewed on Podcasts

For years I've been saying that podcasts are an underutilized opportunity for authors. Unlike traditional radio where guests are often featured for just a few minutes, most podcast shows feature guests for fifteen minutes up to a full hour. There are shows that reach niche audiences, including topics on business, finance, parenting, lifestyles, science, history, true crime, hobbies, and so much more. Podcasts need guests on a daily or weekly basis and the vast majority welcome pitches from authors.

To locate opportunities, search iTunes or Stitcher Radio for podcasts that reach your target audience. Here are some research tips:

- Browse categories that match your audience.
- Type in keywords related to your industry.
- Search authors and influencers in your genre to see who has interviewed them.
- Conduct Google searches for keyword phrases. For example, "small business growth podcast" produces a variety of articles featuring lists of what they deem the top small business podcasts.

I recommend building a spreadsheet with podcast show names that you find. Next, go to Google and locate the website for each show. Many feature "Submission Guidelines" that detail how they want prospective guests to submit a pitch. If guidelines aren't available, look for contact information and send your pitch directly to the host, show producer, or website manager.

Podcast interviews could be one of your most powerful marketing opportunities. Be sure to include this strategy in your marketing plans, especially in the weeks surrounding your book launch.

Sample Podcast Pitch

Greetings <first name>,

Did you know that a recent survey showed that more than eighty percent of Americans would like to write a book? As a publishing industry expert and author of *The Nonfiction Book Publishing Plan*, I would love to be considered as a guest on your program to discuss the current opportunities in publishing and how your listeners can avoid the mistakes many new self-published authors make.

We could also discuss additional topics:

- Simple strategies for writing a book quickly
- The pros and cons of traditional and self-publishing and how to navigate each
- Methods for promoting books online via blogging and social media

I have listened to several of your show's archived episodes and considering your focus on topics for entrepreneurs, I believe we could give your listeners some valuable perspectives they haven't heard anywhere else.

I have over a decade of media experience, so I can assure you that our time together will be well-spent and focused on delivering value to your audience. I have attached my media sheet with sample interview questions and will gladly send you a complimentary copy of my latest book, at your request. I also have a professional microphone and equipment in my home office so I am well-prepared for interviews.

Thank you kindly for your consideration. I look forward to hearing from you soon.

Warm regards,

Stephanie Chandler

<insert contact information: email, phone, website URL, social media links>

Actual Podcast Pitch Used by a PR Firm

In the previous chapter you saw an actual press release sent by Wasabi Publicity on behalf of author Cholet Josué. Here is an email version of that pitch, which was used to reach out to podcasters.

Subject: [Wellness] 3 Brain Tools for a Good Life

Hello <name>,

What can a physician, neuroscientist, and American immigrant success story tell us about the brain tools we need to live our best lives?

I have Dr. Cholet Josué (say sho-LAY jo-ZWAY), a Bahamian Haitian American who shares his top three mental skills we can use to change our lives—even amidst challenging life circumstances.

P.S. Dr. Josué's forthcoming book, *Twelve Unending Summers: Memoir of an Immigrant Child*, will hit bookshelves later this spring.

Read on for details and contact me for interviews.

3 Must-Have Brain Tools for Living Your Best Life

Over the course of his journey from immigrant to neuroscientist, Dr. Josué has discovered the three things he says human beings need to live a good life:

- Financial stability
- Health
- A supportive community

How can people attain these resources? It all starts with accessing the three tools we need to position our brains for success, he says:

- Self-compassion
- Emotional intelligence
- Critical thinking

"If any human being can get these three tools into their brain," Dr. Josué says, "they can get the resources they need to live a good life. My goal is to educate people about their brains, emotions, and behaviors, because that's what governs our lives."

For more information, visit the online press kit at www.choletjosue.onlinepresskit247.com or public website www.drjosue.com.

PART 4

To learn more or to speak with Dr. Cholet Josué, please contact me:

<publicist name, contact information>

Wasabi Publicity

About: Dr. Cholet Kelly Josué is a Bahamian-born Haitian American author and physician seeking a home among the three cultures that have played a role in his life. Born in the Bahamas of Haitian parents who wanted their children to experience their ancestral roots, Cholet moved to Haiti with his siblings when he was four years old. There he spent the next twelve years of his life reveling in a simple and decent, if checkered, childhood until he was sent across the Caribbean Sea in a wooden boat to join his mother in South Florida after the death of his father.

While still an undocumented immigrant, Cholet earned a Bachelor of Science degree in chemistry from Florida Atlantic University. Then he spent the next six months at the University of Miami law library preparing to represent himself in the trial of his life: the quest to become a legal resident.

Cholet received his medical degree from Morehouse School of Medicine in Atlanta, Georgia, and did his residency at the University of Illinois in Chicago. Currently, Cholet practices medicine in the greater Washington, DC, area with a functional and integrative approach and draws on his special interest in behavioral neurology and neuropsychiatry. He is a member of the American Medical Association, the American Psychiatric Association, the Maryland Psychiatric Association, the American Neuropsychiatric Association, the Cognitive Neuroscience Society, and the Society for Neuroscience.

His forthcoming book is entitled *Twelve Unending Summers: Memoir of an Immigrant Child*. Visit www.drjosue.com.

Contribute to Blogs

Consumers love recommendations, especially when it comes to books, so when a blogger recommends your book, his or her readers will listen. Reaching out to bloggers can lead to some tremendous exposure. Some things to keep in mind when contacting bloggers:

- The top bloggers receive a lot of pitches. You might get better results by pitching mid-level bloggers, who still have loyal readers but aren't quite as inundated with requests.
- Make sure your pitch fits the tone of the blog. If you're asking for a book review, search the blog to see if other book reviews have been featured there. If not, find another angle. Perhaps you could offer up copies of your book as a giveaway promotion or contribute a guest article.

- Get creative and try to create a win-win situation as much as possible. For example, you could offer to feature the blogger on your site in exchange for a mention on her site. Or you could offer to promote the blogger to your social media following.
- Flattery will get you everywhere. Make sure you let bloggers know you enjoy their work and that you're familiar with their content.

Conduct searches on Google to locate blogs in your genre. You can also try some creative search combinations:

- Book review + [genre]
- Book review + [titles of books in your genre]
- Author interview + [genre]
- Author interview + [authors in your genre]
- Book giveaway + [genre]

Conduct a Virtual Book Tour

A virtual book tour is a promotion where you set a specified time, usually two to four weeks, and you put yourself on "tour." The idea is to get blogs and podcasts to feature you each day during your tour stops. Blogs might feature a guest blog post by you or a written interview. In exchange, you can share a link back to the host blog on your own site and across your social media networks.

To create a virtual book tour, start by finding appropriate blog sites and then reach out and ask if they would be interested in featuring you during your tour. Most bloggers are familiar with this concept and many will oblige because the benefits are mutual. It's also a good idea to offer the blog host a complimentary copy of your book. This shows goodwill, plus it may hook the blogger and inspire them to write more about your book.

Connect with Social Media Influencers

Much like bloggers, social media influencers are people with large social media followings. You can find them by searching social media sites directly, including Facebook, Instagram, TikTok, LinkedIn, and Pinterest. You will need to be creative with pitches to these folks, though most likely also have active blogs. Consider offering up a contest suggestion or book giveaway.

Find Opportunities on News Sites

Internet news sites like ThriveGlobal.com, HuffPost.com, or CNN.com offer several opportunities. First, the major news sites operate just like traditional media. They are looking for relevant and timely story pitches. Some also feature bloggers, many who are independent contributors for the news site. You can send a traditional media pitch to the journalists (via email) or reach out to the bloggers.

Either way, you need a good pitch to get their attention. Be sure to check all relevant news sites, especially those that reach your unique audience, for submission guidelines. You might uncover an opportunity that is a perfect match for you.

Get Weekly Media Leads for Authors

The Nonfiction Authors Association features a membership benefit called Media Leads for Authors. Subscribing Authority and VIP members of NFAA receive a list of media leads via email every Friday. These opportunities are primarily focused on bloggers and podcasters, though other outlets are featured here as well, and many members have reported success landing interviews. We would love for you to join our tribe! NonfictionAuthorsAssociation.com/join/.

Inspire Media Pros to Come to You

As you establish authority in your field, reporters, editors, producers, podcasters, and other media professionals will begin to seek you out. While you can and should pursue media opportunities, there are steps you can take to help media pros find you. Here are some ways to make that happen:

Blog often – Frequent blogging (two or more times per week) can improve your site's search rankings and can also be a way to attract media. Journalists often use Google to find sources for stories. When you write about topics in your industry on a regular basis, and therefore demonstrate your authority, media pros will inevitably find you.

Build your platform – The more visibility you gain as an expert in your field, the more chances you will give the media to find you. Whether you build a substantial following as a podcaster, YouTube star, blogger, or social media master, the point is that a solid platform leads to opportunities beyond attracting publishers.

Be seen in the right places online – When you show up as an authority on websites, blogs, radio programs, etc., you can attract other media opportunities. The media pros at top publications and shows follow each other's stories, so if you give an impressive interview in a popular publication or show, there's a good chance you'll get inquiries from others.

Get listed on Amazon – Authors are favorites with media professionals as they frequently search Amazon for interview sources. Get that book done already!

Add a media page to your site – Featuring a media page shows journalists that you are savvy, making it easier for them to cover you for stories.

Power Tip: There is a lot of effort involved in researching contacts, which makes this one of my favorite tasks to outsource to a virtual assistant. If you don't have the time or inclination to do this yourself, consider hiring help.

EXERCISE: Research Online Media Outlets
(Blogs, News Sites, Podcasts)

Contact Name	Media Outlet	Email	Link

PART 4

EXERCISE: Write Media Pitches

☐ Craft a pitch that you can send by email to the online media outlets you identified in the previous exercise.

☐ Write a pitch to bloggers inquiring about interviewing you, reviewing your book, hosting a book giveaway contest, sharing an excerpt from your book, or offering to write a guest post—depending on which opportunities exist on the blog based on your earlier research.

CHAPTER 13

Prepare for Interviews

After giving countless media interviews, learning a few things the hard way, and going through formal media training, I've rounded up some of my favorite tips to make your media appearances shine.

Use These Media Training Tips

Be available when the media calls – Things move quickly in the news world and most of the time reporters and producers are working on a deadline. With this in mind, make it easy for the media to reach you by providing your cell phone number and an email address that gets priority attention. I once missed a HUGE media opportunity when I stayed home with my sick kid and didn't check voice mail until the next day. By then it was too late and they found someone else. Don't let this happen to you!

Know your talking points – In the event that you are interviewed about your book, a new program you have launched, or anything else that is newsworthy, make sure you're clear about what points you want to make. Without a clear plan, your answers could ramble and you risk making mistakes.

Guests are expected to talk in sound bites—which essentially means that thoughtful answers should be conveyed swiftly. If the producer were to edit out bits of your interview for promotional purposes, they'd want to capture information and ideas in short quotes.

For radio and television, there is no editing and everything you say is recorded for all eternity. Consider this incentive to know your key messages, practice them, say them out loud in the car, have your kids interview you at the dinner table—and do whatever it takes to always be ready. Company CEOs and political candidates practice and prepare their messages and so should you!

Be ready for rapid fire – Television news programs move through segments at lightning speed. To get a better understanding of how this works, study the *Today Show* or *Good Morning America*. Guests are typically on for just a few minutes and questions move swiftly. Your answers should be brief and to the point. In fact, you should be speaking in sound bites so that each statement you make could stand on its own. This is where those talking points really come in handy. TV and radio show producers like guests who keep up with the pace, demonstrate their expertise, and show confidence. Preparation in advance will set you up for success.

PART 4

Remember to smile – You don't want to look miserable or tense on camera and if you're on the radio, a smile will radiate through your voice.

Check your facial expressions – Try filming yourself while someone interviews you and study how your face looks. I recently watched back an interview I gave and learned the meaning of the term "resting bitch face!" Even after all these years and countless media interviews, I didn't realize that what feels like concentration to me can look like anger to the audience. I was mortified. I've since committed to monitoring my expressions for every interview going forward.

Dress appropriately – If you're on TV, it is best to wear solid, bright colors. Prints and patterns don't translate well on TV. Also, when interviewing in person, whether with a reporter for the local paper or a major news channel, it's always better to be overdressed than underdressed. For women, makeup should be applied slightly heavier than usual since the lighting can wash you out.

Avoid selling – Landing a media interview is not a license to sell. It's a give-more-than-take situation and you walk a fine line when promoting your book. Beware of coming off like you're giving a sales pitch. Instead, work some examples into your talking points like, "In the book, I talk at length about XYZ." Though you want to get the most from your media appearance, you also don't want to give the producers—or the audience—the impression that you are just there to sell.

Be the ultimate interviewee – An interview with a print journalist isn't as high-pressure as a live TV or radio interview, but it can hold just as much value. The journalist may have a set list of questions to ask you when he calls and then midway through the interview he could change things up if he decides to take a different slant for the story. Go with the flow while being professional and gracious.

In some cases, you can actually help shape the story. Remember, you are the authority on the subject matter. If the reporter's approach isn't quite right, you can gently suggest covering the story from a different angle, which could end up being a win-win situation for both of you.

Ask questions – You have the right to ask when the story is going to run and for a copy of the article or video clip for your website. You should know that some media outlets will either charge you to reprint the story on your own site or forbid you from publishing it altogether. If that is the case, you can still mention your appearance and link to the story if it's available online.

Make a lasting impression – When you give a good interview, you increase your odds of being interviewed by the same outlet again in the future. To really be memorable, send a thank-you note after the interview. Not enough people take this crucial step, which will help you be a memorable contributor. You can also touch base with the producer or reporter again months down the road to remind them that you are available for interviews. Better yet, send along another interesting story pitch and a reminder about your previous appearance. Make their jobs easier by becoming a trusted, go-to source and you will build media relationships that can be leveraged again and again.

Be an In-Demand Guest for Radio and Podcasts

Being invited as a guest on a radio show or podcast is an honor and if you want to dazzle the audience and the host, there are some simple guidelines you can follow to ensure your interview is a success.

Let the host lead – Your job as a guest is to make the host look good. That means following the host's lead at all times. Avoid talking over your host. Be patient and wait for questions. Never offend or talk down to the host. Instead, be gracious and professional at all times.

Talk in sound bites –To get an idea about how this works, listen to interviews on popular podcasts or radio programs. As a guest, your answers to interview questions should be brief and to the point.

To shine as a radio guest, be mindful of time. Avoid going on and on in interviews and instead keep your answers to a few sentences or less unless the question warrants a longer response. There is often more leeway on podcasts, especially if you're the featured guest for thirty minutes or more, but you should still make sure you're sticking to the topic at hand and keeping pace with the host.

Tell stories – When asked questions by your host, make the interview more interesting by giving thoughtful examples and real-life stories. You can do this by sharing stories from your own experiences or examples from your book. Storytelling can captivate an audience and contribute to an excellent interview. Plan the stories you want to share prior to your interview so that you come across polished and prepared.

Pace yourself – Talking too fast can be overwhelming for listeners and talking too slow can hurt the pace of the interview. Pay attention to your pace.

Have a conversation – The best interviews are the ones that aren't forced. Talk to the host as if you're talking to a friend. That rapport and camaraderie can translate into an excellent and entertaining interview for listeners.

Never, never, never sell – As a guest, your job is to entertain and inform the audience. The show is not there so that you can give a commercial; otherwise you would be paying for placement. If you make the interview all about your book, you'll never be asked back. Worse, you will turn off the audience.

Be prepared for the close – Oftentimes the host will ask where the audience can learn more about you. This is your chance to give your website address along with a call to action. For example, you might offer listeners a special bonus if they log onto your website and sign up for your mailing list or share a special coupon code valid that day only.

It's a good idea to run promotion ideas by the host or producer ahead of time. For example, you might want to give away a special report to all listeners who sign up for your email list. If that's the case, make sure to ask first so you don't cross any lines. You might also partner with the show to do some kind of book giveaway to listeners. This gives the host added incentive to promote your book and makes it fun for the audience.

Practice – If you're just getting started with radio interviews, enlist a friend to do some mock interviews with you. Nothing removes fear like preparation. This will also help you sound like a seasoned pro when it's time to do the real thing.

Take a deep breath – Your first few interviews may seem a little scary, but with practice it will get much easier. The audience can't see you; so you can sit at your desk with notes all around you (place your sample interview questions with answers front and center). Nobody will be the wiser.

Remember to treat interviews like a conversation. Take a deep breath and have fun with it. Don't forget to prepare beforehand. If you've prepared interview questions and answers, you've won half the battle. When it's all over, you'll realize that you were more prepared than you thought.

Bonus tip – Have a glass of water with a straw nearby (minus the ice since it can make noise) during interviews since your mouth will get dry when doing a lot of talking.

Get Equipment for At-Home Interviews

- ☐ Web camera – Logitech is a popular choice
- ☐ Flexible tripod to adjust camera angle
- ☐ A separate tripod for interviews on your phone
- ☐ Good lighting – a selfie light or simple desk lamp pointed at your face
- ☐ Microphone – Blue Yeti or Audio Technica
- ☐ iPhone with cordless earbuds can be an alternative to the above
- ☐ Thoughtful background, even if it's just a curtain

EXERCISE: Prepare Answers to Interview Questions

Using the interview questions you prepared in chapter 11, write out how you will answer each question. Remember to speak in sound bites and make your answers memorable.

Next, read your answers out loud and practice them over and over again until your key points are committed to memory. This is what the pros (and politicians) do and will ensure you are polished and succinct when in the media hot seat.

PART 5

Boost Sales on Amazon

Favorite Tools

Here are some of my favorite resources that help me run my business.

Squareup.com – Enables easy credit card processing on your mobile devices, which is useful when selling books or other products at events. It also offers digital invoicing and other helpful features.

Zoom.us – We've used Zoom for many years and one benefit to come from pandemic life is that online events will continue to gain popularity. Zoom offers two different options: Meetings and Webinars. Zoom Meetings allows all participants to be seen on screen but limits the number of attendees to 100 unless you purchase an upgrade. Zoom Webinars function like a broadcast where the only people seen on screen are the presenters. Attendees are off-camera and can participate by typing in the Chat or Q&A boxes. We use both formats for a variety of purposes. You should know that these features require two different subscriptions.

Stamps.com – While you can trek down to the post office and surf Facebook while standing in line, or you can print your own postage off the USPS website, Stamps.com makes the process much easier. It provides robust options, including the ability to print UPS shipping labels. There is a small monthly fee, but if you do a fair amount of shipping, it can be worthwhile. And if this is the case, I also recommend buying an inexpensive thermal laser printer specifically for printing labels. It makes life much easier!

Google Sheets, Docs, and Forms – These free tools from Google allow you to create spreadsheets and documents you can share with your team members or clients. Google Forms makes it easy to create applications and other types of submittable forms.

Dropbox – We use Dropbox for all kinds of file sharing between team members and clients. You can also use Dropbox to backup your files and access them from remote locations.

Carbonite – Every single reader of this book should have a backup solution for your computer system. Carbonite is easy and affordable, storing copies of all your files at a remote location so that in the event your computer/laptop is stolen, broken, or dropped out the car window (not a good day), you can restore all your data. This tool is truly essential.

Launch and Optimize Your Book on Amazon

There is no denying that Amazon is an essential tool for book sales. The online behemoth is estimated to command between fifty to seventy percent of all book sales in the world and generates around seventy-five percent of all ebook sales.

According to Markinblog.com, adult nonfiction book sales have grown by twenty-two percent in the past five years. The top five selling categories for hard copy books on Amazon.com are:

1. Memoirs and Biographies
2. Self-Help
3. Religion and Spirituality
4. Health, Fitness, and Dieting
5. Politics and Social Science

The most popular nonfiction categories for e-books on Amazon:

1. Religion and Spirituality
2. Biographies and Memoirs
3. Business and Money
4. Self-Help
5. Cookbooks and Food

Regardless of what genre you write for, if you want to sell more books, it is essential to focus on developing a strong presence on Amazon.

Most authors get their books on Amazon either through distribution by a traditional publisher or through print on demand (POD) publishing services like KDP, Lulu, or IngramSpark. POD services print and fulfill book orders directly to Amazon. If you're self-published and not working with a POD book distributor, you would need to set up an Amazon Seller account at sellercentral.amazon.com.

Understand Sales Rank on Amazon

Every book on Amazon has a sales rank number located near the publisher information. This rating indicates how well the book is selling at that moment in time. It may seem counterintuitive, but the lower the sales rank, the more copies of the book have sold that day.

As an author, it's helpful to monitor sales trends for your books, especially if you have active marketing and publicity campaigns. If an article comes out about you in an industry magazine or you're a featured guest on a podcast, your book's sales rank can show a resulting spike in sales. Sales ranking is recalculated throughout the day, so the rank you see for your book at 9:00 a.m. will be different from its ranking at 5:00 p.m.

While Amazon doesn't publish information about how it tabulates book sales ranking numbers, many authors have speculated over the years about how the ranking system correlates to the number of copies sold based on our own experiences.

Following are *estimated* average book sales based on the ranking.

Estimated Sales Rank and Number of Books Sold Per Day:

100k or higher = **Less than 1 book sold per day**

50,000 to 100k = **1 to 5 books per day**

10,000 to 50,000 = **5 to 20 books per day**

1,000 to 10,000 = **20 to 100 books per day**

100 to 1,000 = **100 to 350 books per day**

20 to 100 = **350 to 800 books per day**

10 to 20 = **800 to 1,200 books per day**

1 to 10 = **1,200+ books per day**

Don't Fear Amazon's Used Book Marketplace

Authors often wonder why their books appear on Amazon under the Used Books category, especially if the book was only recently released. There are legitimate reasons for this.

Most books are distributed through Ingram, the world's largest supplier of books to bookstores. When new titles are released and available through Ingram, independent booksellers can offer them for sale, and purchase them at the wholesale discount you set for your book.

When your book is released into the wild, you will likely find it available for sale with many independent booksellers—across Amazon and even on independent bookseller websites. This can be pretty exciting, though unfortunately that doesn't mean the booksellers have actually *purchased* your book—yet. If and when they generate a sale for your book, they will then purchase the book through Ingram and drop-ship it to the buyer. Yes, this means they can list your book for sale without having a single copy in inventory. They can also list it for sale at any price they choose, whether higher or lower than your chosen retail price.

Many of these indie booksellers will attempt to beat Amazon's available retail price in hopes of capturing the sale. The good news is that regardless of who ends up selling your book, you are still compensated based on sales through Ingram.

Copies of your book may also be listed for sale by individual readers. These could be people who bought your book or somehow acquired a copy. You will not be compensated for used book sales. And this is a good reminder on review copies that you send out for free. Always mark "Review Copy, Not for Resale" to prevent those from ending up in the used book marketplace.

On the upside, you can think of used books like library books. Once a copy of your book is purchased by a library, it can be shared over and over again. Though you won't be paid by those borrowers, each reader can potentially become a fan who visits your website and invests in your other books, products, and services.

Pro Tip: When your share a link to your book with friends, peers, or your audience at large, don't just copy and paste whatever shows up in your browser. Find the short link for your book on Amazon.

Example:

Good link has book title and inventory number:

https://www.amazon.com/Nonfiction-Book-Publishing-Plan-Self-Publishing/dp/1949642003/

Bad link has erroneous text:

https://www.amazon.com/Nonfiction-Book-Publishing-Plan-Self-Publishing/dp/1949642003/ref=sr_1_1?dchild=1&keywords=stephanie+chandler%27&qid=1602599274&sr=8-1

You don't want your link to include erroneous code, so copy the link with the book title and product number only. Be sure to paste it in a browser to test it before sharing with others.

Host a Soft Launch

When your book is traditionally published, you will have little or no control over how it's released on Amazon. But when you self-publish a book, you have several options for introducing it to the world. You can host a presale on Amazon and promote it for weeks or even months in advance. This strategy can be effective if you have a following of supporters and want to build sales momentum.

PART 5

You can also decide to launch your book and hit the ground running, though this strategy can backfire if you promote the book on the same day it's released and you haven't yet worked out the kinks. Amazon can be glitchy and a bit frustrating, so your book may not be ready for *prime* time (no pun intended) right out of the gate.

I often recommend a soft launch strategy for newly published books, which can be surprisingly simple and effective.

Understand a Soft Launch

A soft launch means you quietly release your book on Amazon *without telling anyone*. This gives you some time to work out any potential issues with Amazon and get prepared to dazzle readers.

When you release your book to Amazon, it will populate your book page in increments. This means you might see your book cover and no description, or a description and no cover. Sometimes it takes a few days until all data is populated properly.

Amazon may also show shipping delays on new titles or worse, run out of stock after only a few copies have been sold. To avoid this issue, place an order yourself and ask a couple of friends to do the same.

While waiting for your book page data to update, you can accomplish some important tasks:

1. **Set up your Author Central account.** Login to authorcentral.amazon.com and create your author profile. Here you can upload your photo, share your bio, and post a link to your website. You can also claim your book as the author and update data on your book page. This means you can reformat the book description or extend it by adding more details, post any editorial reviews your book receives, and share a note from the author to potential readers.

2. **Order your book.** Make sure your book is shipping properly, while also starting to create some sales history. Ideally, you should order both the print and Kindle editions to confirm everything arrives as expected.

3. **Generate book reviews.** Before you announce your book to the world, ask a few early readers to post reviews. However, be careful with this strategy because Amazon doesn't like to see a flurry of reviews at once and may ban some users if this happens. It is best to ask friends one by one. And while anyone can post a review on Amazon provided they've spent $50 on the site in the past year—and even if they haven't purchased the book—ask them to buy the book first. This allows the review to show as "verified purchase" and gives the review more legitimacy.

   If your reviewers received early copies of the manuscript to review, you should recommend they post a disclaimer: "I received early access to this book in exchange for my honest review." This will keep their reviews in accordance with Amazon's terms of service. Also note that according to Amazon's terms, you cannot offer incentive for reviews. This means you can't offer to thank reviewers by giving them a bonus of any kind.

4. **Launch Amazon ads.** One of the most effective sales strategies we've seen for nonfiction books is utilizing Amazon ads to gain exposure and generate sales. Mark Paul, author of *The*

Greatest Gambling Story Ever Told: A True Tale of Three Gamblers, the Kentucky Derby, and the Mexican Cartel, sold over thirty thousand copies of his memoir in its first year using nothing but Amazon ads. Amazon ads are covered in chapter 16.

Host a Presale

IngramSpark allows authors/publishers to set up presales on Amazon weeks or even months in advance of your book's official release date. Oddly enough, KDP does *not* currently offer presales for print books; however, you can set up a presale for the Kindle edition of your book. Note that you must have your book files print-ready to do this.

When you set up a presale, you can set a release date in the future and begin pre-promotion efforts. A presale allows readers to commit to purchase the book when it is officially released, and all those preorders are billed on the day your book comes out. In the meantime, if your book sells well in preorder status, it can be highlighted in Amazon bestseller lists, including "Hot New Releases" and other categories where your book is listed. Getting featured on these lists can help raise visibility and boost book sales.

A presale campaign can also help generate reviews quickly since you will have built anticipation with readers ahead of the release date. They will receive the book as soon as it's available and be anxious to crack it open.

You can host a presale campaign for any length of time you like. I recommend no more than a few weeks, though, to keep your audience engaged and excited about the release.

Manage E-book Presales

In addition to setting up your print book for presale, you can create preorders for your Kindle and other e-book editions. Preorders for Kindle should be set up directly via kdp.amazon.com. For preorders on other e-book platforms, including Apple iBooks, Barnes and Noble Nook, and Kobo, you can set up distribution with Draft2Digital.

You may want to setup your preorder campaign at least four weeks in advance to create merchandising opportunities with retailers. For example, each week Apple promotes its top-selling preorders, and getting your book listed here can inspire more sales. Smashwords also recommends that authors with previously published titles should update the back matter of your previous e-books to indicate the on-sale date for your new book. This will not only help readers find your new title, but it may help retailers cross-promote your new e-book with buyers of your previous e-books.

Note that Amazon Kindle requires you to have a fully formatted e-book file uploaded to participate in preorders. Draft2Digital allows authors at any stage, whether with a completed file or an "asset-less" preorder, to schedule a preorder campaign up to a full year in advance. Just like with your print book, your e-books will go live on retailer sites on the date you choose.

PART 5

Optimize Your Book for Better Amazon Placement

Like it or not, we all must put focused effort and attention into selling on Amazon and understanding how it works since most book sales happen there. Many independent authors have a love-hate relationship with Amazon due to their policies and business practices that aren't exactly friendly to publishers.

Think of Amazon as a giant search engine, which is exactly how most people use the site. For example, when you type in a search for "book about climate change" or "how to raise farm animals," Amazon returns what it deems to be the most relevant results. And those results are based on technology called *algorithms.*

Though Amazon doesn't publicly share how its algorithms calculate search results, those of us who've been around for a while have come to our own conclusions based on what we've seen and experienced. It's widely believed that Amazon's algorithms factor in the following:

- Recent sales history
- Click-through rates
- Conversion rates
- Number of reviews
- Keywords used in search

Recent Book Sales History

Like any retailer, Amazon wants to make money; therefore, it pays attention to what books are selling well and gives those titles higher priority over competing titles. The more book sales you generate, the more Amazon will help boost sales by cross-promoting your book with other titles and giving it a higher position in search results. Yes, this can be frustrating because it requires that you drive sales yourself. But if you're doing the work and leading buyers to your book, Amazon will reward your efforts with increased promotion on the site.

Click-Through Rates

Amazon tracks how many times a product appears in search results and how many times a shopper clicks on that product. If your book appears in search results but isn't generating enough clicks, that can impact future search results. This means that your book cover and title need to appeal to readers and inspire them to click through to your book page.

Conversion Rates

When someone clicks on your book and then makes a purchase, that is considered a conversion. When you have a higher-than-average conversion rate for book sales, Amazon will factor this in.

And when visitors to your book page don't buy, Amazon notices this too. You can help by ensuring you have an excellent book description, professional cover design, positive reader reviews, and a compelling author bio.

Number of Book Reviews

Book reviews show Amazon that your book is popular and liked by readers, provided reviews are mostly positive. Some believe that reaching a certain number of reviews (somewhere between fifty and ninety) triggers Amazon's algorithms and improves visibility for the book. All we know for sure is that reviews influence potential readers to buy books, so your goal should always be to generate as many reviews as possible on an ongoing basis.

Note that a review from someone who purchased your book from Amazon is denoted as a "verified purchase" and holds more weight than other reviews—not just with Amazon, but with readers too. See chapter 15 for tips on how to land book reviews.

Keywords on Amazon

When you set up your book for distribution, you will have the ability to identify specific keyword phrases that describe your book, also known as metadata. Consider what terms your target audience would use to find your book. Also, as much as possible, incorporate top keywords into your book's title or subtitle for best results. Choose keywords carefully, as they can have a big impact on search results.

I searched Amazon for "guide to running" and these are the top results I received, in the order that they appeared:

- *The Young Entrepreneur's Guide to Starting and Running a Business: Turn Your Ideas into Money!* By Steve Mariotti
- *Relentless Forward Progress: A Guide to Running Ultramarathons* by Bryon Powell, Patrick Lawlor, et al.
- *The Butler's Guide to Running the Home and Other Graces* by Stanley Ager and Fiona St. Aubyn
- *Running Randomized Evaluations: A Practical Guide* by Rachel Glennerster and Kudzai Takavarasha
- *Legal Guide for Starting and Running a Small Business* by Fred S. Steingold and David Steingold

Clearly Amazon's algorithms aren't as precise as we'd like to believe. It's also likely this eclectic list of search results also factored in previous search history since I read a lot of business books. But let this serve as a warning that *keywords matter.* Also note that you can and should incorporate keyword phrases into the description for your book.

PART 5

Categories

The categories where your book is listed can have a major impact on sales. For example, if your book is about running marathons, but it isn't listed in Amazon's Running and Jogging category, it may miss out on purchases from people who browse that category.

When you publish a print book and distribute to Amazon, you can indicate three suggested categories for your book based on BISAC codes (Book Industry Standards and Communications), which are managed by the Book Industry Study Group (BISG). BISAC codes help libraries and bookstores know where to shelve your books. See codes here: bisg.org/page/BISACSubjectCodes.

Amazon has thousands of its own categories, well beyond standard BISAC codes. Their algorithms ultimately determine categories for your book, which may or may not align with your suggested BISAC categories. You can locate the categories assigned to any book by scrolling down a book page on Amazon and looking next to the publisher information. Following is from the paperback version of *Girl Walks Out of a Bar: A Memoir* by Lisa F. Smith.

Product details

Publisher : SelectBooks (June 7, 2016)

Language : English

Paperback : 288 pages

ISBN-10 : 1590793218

ISBN-13 : 978-1590793213

Reading age : 18 years and up

Item Weight : 14.5 ounces

UNSPSC-Code : 55101500

Dimensions : 5.9 x 0.7 x 8.9 inches

Best Sellers Rank: #22,661 in Books (See Top 100 in Books)
  #89 in Alcoholism Recovery
  #409 in Women's Biographies
  #1,307 in Memoirs (Books)

Customer Reviews: ★★★★☆ ⌄   1,021 ratings

The Kindle edition of *Girl Walks Out of a Bar* is assigned to slightly different categories:

Product details

ASIN : B01G12I6SI

Publisher : SelectBooks (June 7, 2016)

Publication date : June 7, 2016

Language : English

File size : 1663 KB

Text-to-Speech : Enabled

Screen Reader : Supported

Enhanced typesetting : Enabled

X-Ray : Enabled

Word Wise : Enabled

Print length : 288 pages

Lending : Enabled

Best Sellers Rank: #49,710 in Kindle Store (See Top 100 in Kindle Store)
  #36 in Alcoholism (Kindle Store)
  #121 in Alcoholism Recovery
  #203 in Biographies & Memoirs of Women

Customer Reviews: ★★★★⯪ ⌄   1,021 ratings

How to Update Amazon Categories

For many years, Amazon has allowed authors to request their books be listed in up to ten Amazon categories. The biggest benefit of being listed in multiple categories is that it can improve the discoverability of your book, especially when your book sells enough copies to appear in the top ten of a category. So, when potential readers scroll through the category where your book is listed in the top sellers, the odds of your book being purchased increase greatly. Discoverability on Amazon is everything when it comes to attracting new readers.

In addition, when your book reaches #1 status in any category, it earns the bestseller tag, and the tag stays there *while the book is in that position*. See Mark Paul's book *The Greatest Gambling Story Ever Told*:

To be clear, the goal here is NOT to reach bestseller status for five minutes so you call your book an Amazon bestseller. I do NOT condone this as a marketing practice.

There is no long-term value of having a bestselling book in a small category on Amazon for an hour or a day. However, there is tremendous value in *remaining in the number one position of a category over the long term* because of the best seller designation and improved discoverability of your book. And if you can't be in the number one spot, at least aim to hover in the top ten of at least one category for months or even years.

Amazon Limits the Number of Categories for Books

In 2023, Amazon changed its policies, no longer allowing authors to request a book be listed in up to ten categories. Now, you can only choose a maximum of three categories, which means you must choose your categories carefully. Do not let Amazon automatically choose the categories for you because they will likely get them wrong.

How to Locate Your Book's Categories for Your Print and Ebook

If you have one or more books available for sale on Amazon, it's imperative that you check each edition of your book on Amazon to see in which categories your book is listed.

Categories are listed on your book's sales page on Amazon, about halfway down the page below "Bestsellers Ranks."

I checked the categories for my book, *The Nonfiction Book Publishing Plan*. The Kindle edition is listed in the following categories:

Best Sellers Rank: #230,038 in Kindle Store (See Top 100 in Kindle Store)

    #6 in Electronic Publishing

    #7 in Writing Skills in Advertising

    #147 in Authorship

Customer Reviews: 4.7 ⭐⭐⭐⭐½ ⌄   199 ratings

The only category I would question here is "Writing Skills in Advertising," which is an odd choice. But because the book is ranked highly there, I need to decide if I want to keep that category or choose another relevant category where the book can also rank well.

How to Choose Categories on Amazon Manually

Once you've identified a list of current categories for each edition of your book, next you will want to see what other categories may be available within your genre. You can do this by looking up competing book titles and seeing what categories they are listed in.

Each time you discover a new category, click the link to open it in a new window. If there are perennial favorites that could stay there for a long time, making it hard to advance your book to the top ten, you may want to look for another category with less competition.

Category selection is tricky, especially when doing it manually. But this is an important step all authors should take.

How to Choose Categories with Publisher Rocket

Publisher Rocket is software you can purchase, currently for under $100. This is an excellent tool for locating categories and keywords. It identifies all the related Amazon categories and shows you how competitive it is to get your book into the top ten of each category. If you want to make this task easier, you may want to invest in this tool: https://bit.ly/pubrocket-nfaa. (Affiliate link)

How to Request Category Changes in KDP

If your book is published with KDP, you can now make the changes directly from your dashboard. Go to "Edit book details" and scroll down to the "Choose Categories" field. You will see a drop-down menu where you can begin selecting your categories. Follow the steps to add three categories. After a few days, check your listing to see if your category changes have been incorporated.

PART 5

How to Request a Change in Categories for Your Non-KDP Book

If your book is published outside of KDP, you can request category changes through your free Author Central account. In my experience, Author Central support often responds faster than the KDP support team anyway so I recommend starting here with all kinds of Amazon support requests.

Login to your Author Central account and scroll down to the bottom of the page. Locate the "Contact Us" link and click on it. You will be taken to a screen where you indicate why you need support. Select "Amazon Book Page," and then choose "Update Amazon Categories." Follow the prompts to complete your request.

What Next?

Once your categories are updated properly, keep an eye on your book's sales rankings. These are tabulated several times throughout each day so what you see in the morning may be different in the evening. Remember, the goal is NOT to be at the top of a category for a hot minute! It's to hover in the top ten of one or more relevant categories for the long term.

EXERCISE: Incorporate Keyword Phrases

If you have a book on Amazon now, identify top keyword phrases your readers would use to find your book, then incorporate them into your book description on the site.

Understand the KDP Select Program

The KDP Select program is available to Kindle e-book publishers and allows authors and publishers to participate in special advertising campaigns. To enroll in KDP Select, Amazon requires that you give them exclusive distribution rights to your e-book. This means that you cannot distribute your e-book via the Barnes and Noble Nook, iBookstore, Smashwords, etc. In fact, you can't even sell your e-book directly through your own website. This is also one of those policies that frustrate independent authors and publishers because it's Amazon's way of trying to monopolize the e-book market.

The KDP Select program offers several options.

Price Promotions

This is one of the most popular KDP Select features because it allows authors the option to make their Kindle e-books available for free or at a low cost, such as $0.99 (Kindle Countdown Deals), for a brief period of time. This can be a useful strategy *for fiction authors* who write series books. Getting the first book in a series into as many readers' hands as possible can lead to sales of other books in the series.

For nonfiction authors, this program rarely holds much value, unless you have numerous titles and perhaps want to bring new life to an old backlist title.

Kindle Unlimited and Kindle Lending Library

When you enroll your e-book in Kindle Unlimited and/or the Kindle Lending Library, readers who participate in these programs can read your Kindle e-book for free. You will then be paid based on the percentage of the book read. Payments are distributed from a global fund that Amazon creates each month to compensate its authors.

Payments earned with these programs are lower than if you were to sell the book outright, but Amazon insists that you can reach more potential readers by participating. The theory is that readers who wouldn't otherwise find or purchase your book will be more likely to read it because they can access it for free with their Amazon Prime membership. Note that you can also enroll in Kindle Unlimited and the Kindle Lending Library in other countries.

I feel that this program better serves fiction authors who want to reach a bigger audience since avid fiction readers tend to participate in programs on Amazon where they can access an abundance of free and low-cost titles. Nonfiction readers, especially for niche titles, tend to choose books based on the topic as opposed to casual browsing or price promotions.

Royalties

The KDP Select program touts that participants receive increased royalties earned on e-book sales in India, Brazil, and Mexico. Instead of earning thirty-five percent royalties, you'll earn seventy percent. This might matter to you if you generate an incredible number of sales in these countries, but that is unusual.

Should You Enroll in KDP Select?

Consider the following questions:

- Would giving your book away for free lead to more sales? (It's certainly possible that word of mouth from readers could ultimately help lead to more sales, though when readers download free books, they aren't always motivated to read them right away, or ever.)
- Do you believe price promotions can boost sales enough to make it worthwhile, even though you won't be able to distribute your e-book elsewhere?
- Is your book the first in a series? If so, this may work well for you.
- Do you believe the Kindle Unlimited program and Kindle Lending Library can lead to more readers and increased sales?

Bottom line: If KDP Select intrigues you, you can try it out for a few months. If it doesn't produce the results you hoped for, you can opt out of the program and proceed with distributing your e-book on other platforms.

Create Bestseller Campaigns that Last for Months (Not an Hour or a Day)

Many authors have a goal of getting their books on Amazon's various bestseller lists. Amazon has thousands of book categories and subcategories, and because book sales ranks are tabulated hourly, it's not difficult for a book to end up in the top ten of titles within a small subcategory on the site.

Unfortunately, this approach has eroded the term "bestselling author." All it takes is convincing everyone you know to buy your book on a single day. Do this well and voilà! You can end up on an Amazon bestseller list. But is this really something you want to shout from the rooftops?

Several years ago, I worked with an author who spent thousands of dollars hiring a company to hold an Amazon bestseller campaign for the launch of her financial advice guide. The company she hired reportedly enlisted dozens of other authors to announce the book to their networks via email and social media on launch day, with the goal of driving sales to Amazon.

As the day went on, the book moved up the ranks until it reached the number two position in its tiny subcategory:

Books > Computers & Technology > Networking & Cloud Computing > Cloud Computing

That afternoon, the author called to ask how many books had sold so far. She was excited to write a big fat check to her favorite charity based on the results of her book sales.

Guess how many copies sold that day?

A grand total of thirty books.

The company the author had paid thousands of dollars to probably bought at least half of the copies (15 copies x $20 = $300, less than ten percent of the author's investment in those services), and the author's friends probably bought the other half. After the initial launch day, the book fell back off the top of the category list, and never landed there again.

Should You Host an Amazon Best Seller Campaign?

While generating sales on a single day can get your book in the top ten list of a subcategory on Amazon, there is virtually no long-term value. Once the promotion is over, books fall right off the list unless you keep the promotion wheels in motion.

With that said, being at the top of a list is fun and it does give you bragging rights. Just keep your expectations in check. It won't likely take as many sales as you think to reach the top of a small subcategory. Yet, while your book is there, it will raise exposure with potential readers who browse that category, which can ultimately lead to even more sales.

We all want to have a buzz-worthy book launch and come out of the gate with a solid promotional campaign. Whether you make it to a best sellers list or not, you will certainly gain some satisfaction from a job well-done. Hopefully, you will also rack up some book reviews too.

Rather than focusing on reaching the top of a category for one day (or one hour) and claiming bestseller status, I urge you to focus on staying at the top of your chosen category for the long-term. This can absolutely be accomplished. It takes ongoing marketing effort, which should be the goal for any author who cares about generating book sales anyway. And when your book hovers in the top ten titles of a category, it will absolutely create more visibility for the book and should lead to increased sales.

By the way, Amazon also pays attention to buyers, so you won't be able to game the system. Don't bother ordering fifty or five hundred copies of your book, because that bulk purchase won't count. And forget about creating dozens of Amazon accounts and ordering your books that way either. Amazon tracks IP addresses and credit cards and will not count those orders.

PART 5

Did you know?

The Nonfiction Book Awards is a year-round program honoring the best in nonfiction. Books are not judged against competing titles but are reviewed by our judges based on a scoring system that evaluates the quality of the writing and production of the book (editing, design, and other details). A book can receive a bronze, silver, or gold award based on the final evaluation score.

As with other reputable awards programs, not all books receive a Nonfiction Book Award. However, books that are well-written and professionally produced often qualify for a bronze, silver, or gold award.

Winning a Nonfiction Book Award is like adding a seal of approval to your book. It tells readers and media professionals that you have a high-quality book worth reading!

Learn more: NonfictionBookAwards.com

CHAPTER 15

Set Up Author Central and Get More Book Reviews

mazon's Author Central program is a free resource for authors. When you set up an account, you create an author profile on Amazon which is linked to your book's sales page. Your profile includes your bio along with links to your website, social media, and your blog feed.

Put Your Author Central Account to Work

Author Central allows you to monitor your book sales activity and book reviews. Most importantly, you can update the information on your book page on Amazon at any time. This means you can—and should—expand your book description to incorporate relevant keyword phrases. Author Central is a powerful tool and I strongly recommend you take full advantage of its features.

Claim Your Book

As soon as your book is published and available on Amazon (whether self-published or traditionally published, it works the same), go to Author.Amazon.com and log in with your existing Amazon user ID and password. (If you aren't already an Amazon customer, you will need to create an account.)

Once there, click on the "Books" tab and then the "Add a Book" button. Follow the prompts to search for your book by your name or title, and then claim it for your author profile. Repeat these steps for your print and e-book editions.

Profile Tab

Add the following elements to your author profile:

- **Biography** – This should be an overview of your professional experience as it relates to your book(s). Write several paragraphs and include your website link at the end. (Many authors forget to include their website. Make this a habit anytime you share a biography publicly.)

- **Photo** – Upload a professional author photo. This will be featured on your book's page on Amazon and in search results for your name.

Books Tab

Here you will see your books listed. Click a book cover and then "Edit Book Details" to make changes to the content on your book's page. You can update the description, add editorial reviews, and add a note from the author. This is an opportunity to incorporate your most important keywords into your book's sales page.

Important note when updating your book: at the top of the screen to the right of your book image and publisher data, Amazon will list whether the information is listed for the print edition or Kindle. Changes made to one will *not* populate to the other, so you need to make changes on both.

Reports and Marketing Tab

This tab allows you to monitor your book sales history.

- **Nielsen BookScan** – Nielsen is the industry's leading source for tracking book sales from retailers beyond Amazon, including brick-and-mortar bookstores—though it admits to only capturing about seventy percent of print book sales from retailers outside of Amazon. However, I find their tracking is fairly accurate for authors who sell most of their books online, and it's a good resource for monitoring sales activity. You can also view sales by geography so you can see the cities where you've generated the most sales.
- **Sales Rank** – The sales rank trends for your book(s) over time.
- **Customer Reviews** – Here you will see a listing of all reviews of your book, which is extra helpful if you've authored multiple titles because you can check to see if new reviews have been posted. You may also want to contact past reviewers when you release your next book so that you can offer them review copies. This gives you a handy place to find them.
- **Book Recommendations** – This feature allows you to choose books you want to recommend to your readers. Those books will appear on your author profile. This can be an opportunity to cross-promote with fellow authors or simply show readers some books that have made an impact for you.

Overall, it's a good idea to pop into your Author Central account periodically so you can monitor sales activity and update details for your book and your author bio, which can change with time. Any time you release a new title, you will need to repeat the above steps.

We have a bonus book sales tracking spreadsheet you can download, along with other bonus documents here: http://workbookbonus.com.

Add Graphics to Your Book Page Using A+ Content

Traditional publishers have had the ability to add graphic images and extra content to make their book pages sizzle, so if you're traditionally published, ask your publisher to take full advantage of this cool feature. This feature was finally made available to self-published authors whose books are published through KDP. It's called A+ Content and though the process to add it to your book page is a bit tedious, it can be worth the effort. You can access the A+ Content feature here: kdp.amazon. com/marketing/manager.

This feature can accommodate a variety of image sizes or images combined with text that can be added to your page, though you need to supply your own images and content. You can use this feature to expand on your book's benefits, highlight media appearances or editorial reviews, show charts and graphs, or feature just about anything you think would help convert book browsers into buyers.

Be sure to read the content guidelines so you can follow the process step by step since as mentioned, it's a bit tedious to set-up.

Commit to Boosting Book Reviews

Amazon welcomes reviews for all products because positive reviews help improve sales. Because of this, reviews are allowed from people who didn't purchase a book or product from the site. The only requirement for posting a review on Amazon is that you previously spent at least $50 on Amazon in the past year.

Amazon is constantly updating their policies around book reviews, and they have also been cracking down on reviews that are fake, as well as reviews by people who it deems as having a relationship with the author. The whole process seems rather arbitrary, and it's not worth losing sleep over, but you should know about it. Your friends and family may not be able to post reviews of your book, but as an author, your goal should be to generate reviews from actual readers anyway.

Amazon's guidelines say that authors cannot offer incentive for reviews, but you are allowed to *ask for reviews*. So, you can't tell your audience that you'll give them a bonus or discount in exchange for a review. But you could say, "If you liked the book, I'd appreciate a review on Amazon."

If you provide complimentary ARCs (advance review copies) of your book, it is best to instruct recipients to add a disclaimer to any review they post. It should look something like this: "I received an advance review copy in exchange for my honest review."

Including the disclaimer will ensure nobody violates Amazon's policies. Also note that when a reviewer does purchase the book from Amazon, his or her review will be noted as a "verified purchase." It's important to have reviews that include verified purchases. You don't want it to look like all your reviews came from your friends. This could raise a flag with Amazon as well as potential buyers.

Reviews on Amazon are hugely important to the success of a book. Potential buyers look to reviews to help decide to buy, and Amazon's algorithms factor in the number of reviews a book has generated. The more reviews a book receives, the better the likelihood of that book showing up higher in Amazon search results.

PART 5

Get Book Reviews for Free

Amazon reviewers – Each Amazon book reviewer has a public profile, and many include their email addresses and website information (many top reviewers are also bloggers—for even more exposure). These reviewers WANT to be contacted and offered free review copies! Look for reviewers of competing titles, send an email and ask if he/she would like to receive a review copy of your book.

Industry bloggers – Seek out bloggers who cover topics of interest to your target audience or industry. See if they conduct book reviews, publish book excerpts, or interview authors. As mentioned earlier, Google searches should help you compile a list of bloggers to contact.

Book review bloggers – Bloggers have tremendous influence with readers when it comes to reviewing and recommending books. Search Google for *<genre>* + *"book review."*

Major media bloggers – All of the major magazines and newspapers now host blogs (from the *New York Times* to *Cat Fancy* magazine), and many of those blog posts are written by unpaid contributors. Seek out freelance contributors who cover topics related to your target audience and offer up a review copy.

Email subscribers – Periodically send a note to your mailing list subscribers gently reminding them that book reviews help sell books and that you'd appreciate it if readers would post a review for your book.

Smaller publications – Don't overlook trade association newsletters and magazines, plus smaller magazines and even hometown newspapers.

Your website – Create a Review Copy Request form on your website. Ask visitors to provide you with details, including website link and size of audience, to qualify to receive a complimentary review copy.

Contest on your site – Consider using Rafflecopter, a simple program that you can plug in to your site to host a book giveaway contest—it's free! Gently ask (and remind) contest winners to post reviews after reading.

Online groups – Announce that you are interested in sending out review copies to groups that reach your target audience. You can find all kinds of groups via:

- Facebook
- LinkedIn
- Goodreads
- BookRix

Book clubs – Offering copies to book clubs for free can lead to reviews and buzz for your books. Search for book clubs by genre online and via Meetup.com.

Social media – Invite your audience to become book reviewers. You can share a link to your "Review Copy Request" form on your website or conduct a contest to give away several review copies.

Beta readers – As we covered in chapter 9, giving early access to your manuscript to a select group of readers can be an effective way to generate early book reviews from participants.

Giveaways at events – Whenever you donate copies of your book for raffle prizes or gifts, tuck a note inside the book asking the recipient to post a review.

Peers, clients, family, friends – While you want to be careful asking family and friends to write reviews because you don't want any of your reviews to appear biased, it certainly doesn't hurt to ask the people you know to read your book and share an honest review.

Readers who contact you – As an author, you can expect that your readers will periodically contact you, either via email or social media, to let you know they enjoyed your book. When this happens, always reply with gracious appreciation, and then ask the reader to post a review online.

Get Book Reviews for a Fee

Book Review Targeter – This software program allows you to search for Amazon book reviewers who have reviewed books similar to yours, and then export their email addresses and websites or send them an email right from the software. While you can research reviewers one at a time by yourself, it will take you countless hours to do this manually. Every author needs reviews and Book Review Targeter can make it much easier. Learn more here: https://bit.ly/bookreviews-nfaa (affiliate link).

Book Life – Hosted by *Publishers Weekly*, submit your book for a professional editorial review at BookLife.com.

Goodreads Giveaways – More than 40,000 people enter to win books from Goodreads Giveaways each day. Authors can offer up books or e-books to this program and specify the number of days the promotion will run. An average of 825 people enter to win these promotions. Goodreads selects the winners at the end and sends authors a CSV file with addresses. When mailing copies of books to winners, be sure to insert a note requesting that the recipient write a review if they enjoy the book. Other giveaway sites: LibraryThing and BookLikes.

Note that if your e-book is enrolled in Amazon's KDP Select program, you will not be able to participate in free e-book giveaways, a major downside of the Kindle exclusive distribution clause.

Midwest Book Review – A wonderful organization that supports indie authors, MidwestBookReview.com has been around for many years and its volunteer reviewers assess books for a small fee.

PART 5

NetGalley – For a modest fee, you can list your book in the NetGalley.com directory and make it available to hundreds of thousands of reviewers to choose from. You must first apply to participate in this program and it tends to be fiction-centric like so many other programs, but it can lead to some fresh reviews.

Kirkus – An established and reputable editorial review service, Kirkus.com provides professional-level reviews for a modest fee.

Foreword Magazine – Reputable reviews for indie authors via publishers.forewordreviews.com/.

BookBub – The top service for paid email campaigns to promote free and discounted e-books, BookBub.com maintains massive lists of email subscribers interested in acquiring books by genre. These campaigns don't guarantee reviews, but often lead to them. See also BargainBooksy.com, FreeBooksy.com, and BookSends.com.

EXERCISE: Use This Amazon Reviews To-Do List

- ☐ Send an email to your beta readers asking them to post their reviews.
- ☐ Research reviewers of competing books on Amazon to see if they list an email address or contact information. Offer a review copy.
- ☐ Ask social media followers to post reviews.
- ☐ Get in the habit of asking for reviews. If you receive an email from a reader, reply with a request for a review.
- ☐ Reach out to mailing list subscribers and ask for reviews.
- ☐ Ask peers, past readers, and anyone who received a review copy to post a review.
- ☐ Add a note within your book: "The best way to thank an author is to post a review on Amazon!" You can also have this printed on bookmarks.
- ☐ Consider investing in Netgalley.com, a service that makes the e-book version of your book available to volunteer reviewers.
- ☐ Consider hosting a giveaway on Goodreads, as these can lead to reviews.
- ☐ Follow up with anyone who received a review copy. You may need to remind them to write a review.
- ☐ See the other review resources in this chapter and choose two or three to follow up on.

EXERCISE: Important Amazon Tasks

☐ Check Amazon to confirm that your print, Kindle, and audiobook editions (if applicable) are available for sale before you proceed to announce your book launch. Sometimes it takes several days to iron out the kinks with Amazon before you publicly promote your release.

☐ Verify that your book is listed in the right categories. If you had hoped it would appear in a different category, login to your KDP.Amazon.com account or your Author Central account and contact support. You can send an email asking to have the book added to up to three categories that you provide.

☐ View your book page and confirm all editions (print, Kindle, audiobook) are linked together on one page. If not, go to KDP.Amazon.com and link them together. You can also contact customer support through Author Central, send the ISBNs for each edition, and request that they be linked together.

☐ As soon as your book is available on Amazon, set up your free Author Central account: Author.Amazon.com.

☐ In your Author Central account, go to the Author tab and add your bio, author photo, and a link to your blog feed.

☐ From the Books tab, claim your book as yours. It may take a day for this to get approved by Amazon.

☐ Once your book appears in your Author Central account, you can update details on the book sales page. You can modify the description or clean up its formatting, add editorial reviews, add notes from the author, and more. Add as much detail here as you can, including relevant keyword phrases.

☐ Take advantage of the A+ Content option and add some graphic elements to your book page.

☐ Click on the Sales Info tab and navigate through the menu options. This is where your sales data will appear once your book is officially released.

☐ You can also keep track of user reviews in the Customer Reviews tab. (Note that reviews aren't allowed until the book is officially released.)

Commit to doing
a minimum of three things
each day
to promote your books
and build
your author career.

CHAPTER 16

Utilize Amazon Advertising

Did you know that the books you see on endcaps and display tables at Barnes and Noble are most likely sponsored by the publishers? That's right; books featured are there because publishers pay a premium to get their top titles featured on the best real estate in the big stores. Amazon is now following a similar model with its online store using Amazon Marketing Services.

It has become harder to optimize books to show up in traditional search results on Amazon due to the amount of competition, as well as sponsored titles gaining top placement. Just as Facebook made the shift to being a pay-to-play network, requiring paid advertising to get visibility for posts shared there, Amazon is clearly making a shift in the direction of pay-to-play for book marketing and visibility.

Using this model, Amazon earns money whether a browser buys a book or simply clicks on a sponsored title. It's another revenue-generating machine for the retail giant. But this also means that Amazon wants your ads to succeed because when you succeed, so does Amazon.

Locate Sponsored Ads on Amazon

Sponsored books currently show up in the following places on Amazon:

- **The top of search results.** If you search for "keto cookbook" or "Vietnam war books," the first couple of results are usually sponsored titles.
- **In the middle of search results.** Not only do sponsored books appear at the top of search results, but sponsored titles are sprinkled throughout all search results. A sponsored book can be shown as the seventh or fifteenth or thirtieth book in the list of search results.
- **In the "Products related to this item" sections.** These are found on individual book sales pages.
- **On the lock screen and top of Kindle reader devices.**

What Does This Mean for Authors?

This shift toward pay-to-play advertising means that if you want your book to get more visibility on Amazon, you must pay for that exposure. The good news for authors is that these ads can be quite effective, especially for nonfiction titles.

PART 5

Amazon ads follow a pay-per-click model and range from $0.25 to $2.50 per click, depending on competition for each keyword phrase. When you optimize your ads to target the right potential readers, and if your book's sales page does a good job of converting visitors into buyers, then your small investment in clicks could pay for itself big time.

My feeling is advertising with Amazon is a rather low-risk proposition. You can set a daily budget of as little as $1 and then monitor the results, though I recommend starting with at least $10 per day to accurately test your ads. Remember, once they're performing well, you should earn back your investment, plus additional profit.

Aim for Return on Investment (ROI)

With any kind of advertising, the goal should be to generate a significant Return on Investment (ROI). Ideally, for every dollar spent you would earn back $2 or more in book sales. The goal is always to achieve a profitable return on your investment.

For example, if you earn an average of $5 per book sold, and if you spend $3 in click ads to generate one sale, you'd earn an ROI of $2 and come out ahead. Of course, we all want to earn the highest return on investment possible, though any ROI is better than none at all because it means your book is getting into the hands of readers.

For many nonfiction authors, it's not as much about the revenue earned as it is about getting the word out about your book. Perhaps this means that you wouldn't mind earning just pennies per sale, because you'd still come out ahead by gaining a new reader. You might even be willing to take a loss on ads, because your book itself generates ROI from other business opportunities such as speaking engagements or consulting clients.

Many nonfiction authors rave about their results with Amazon ads and generate lots of book sales. These seem to work especially well for niche titles. Others have reported that results are mediocre at best, though they may not fully understand how to properly set up their ads. As with any kind of marketing, you must test it out to find out what works best for your unique book.

Choose from Two Types of Ads

You have two primary options with Amazon ads:

Automatic targeting – You set a daily budget and allow Amazon to figure out where to place your ads. These are easiest to set up, but also offer the least control over ad placement and performance. For some authors, automatic ads work exceptionally well, though not for all authors. It can be worthwhile to test them out since you won't know until you try. Remember, Amazon wants your ads to perform so their algorithms will work to improve your ad performance.

Manual targeting – You are in the driver's seat with manual targeting ads, which means you choose your keyword phrases and your bid strategy. These ads can perform well but will take some time to get set up and running optimally.

Understand How Keywords Power Amazon Ads

Amazon will display a list of selected keywords that you can add to your campaign if you like. These keywords will likely be broad, and you don't have to select them all. Just choose the ones that fit best.

Look for the link at the top that says, "Add your own keywords." Keyword phrases are recommended over single words since they produce more specific results.

To locate keywords:

- **Consider what readers search for** – Think about what your readers might type in to search for a book like yours. You might use keywords like "single mom memoir," "cancer memoir," "breast cancer memoir," and "how to live with breast cancer."
- **Use book and chapter topics** – If your book is prescriptive nonfiction, consider various topics and chapters covered in your book and add those as keywords. For example, if your book is about holistic health solutions, your keywords might be based on your chapters and include "gluten-free living," "how to meditate," "how to be happy," "how to lose weight," etc.
- **Identify the competition** – Most importantly, list titles of competing books and names of authors who write in your genre. This will help your book appear in search results for those books and authors.

Set-up Ads

Ads are set up from the Advertising dashboard: <u>advertising.amazon.com/</u>. Amazon provides instructions for setting these up and there are a variety of resources available online, including at <u>NonfictionAuthorsAssociation.com</u>. Setup instructions are not included here because the steps change too frequently, but this is something you can certainly do yourself if you are so inclined.

Tips for Adding Keywords

Open a separate browser tab and search Amazon for some of your top keyword combinations. Identify the top competing authors and book titles and then use those for keywords.

It is imperative that you don't skimp on keyword combinations. The more keywords you add, the better chance your ads will get displayed. *Aim for a minimum of fifty keyword phrases*, though one hundred or more is optimal when spread out over multiple ads.

Also, beware of keyword combinations that really don't relate to your book. You wouldn't market a science book to children's book readers, for example, unless there was some sort of science connection.

Poorly targeted keywords can hurt your conversion rates and cost you more in clicks that fail to convert to sales. Try to stick with keywords, book titles, and authors whose books are like yours.

Each time you type in a dozen or so keywords, click "Add." If any of your keywords are not allowed by Amazon, you will get a warning message and will need to remove them before it will allow you to successfully add the rest of the keywords on the screen. It will also warn you if you've already added a keyword. This prevents you from losing all your work if you accidentally close your browser or your internet goes out.

If you want to prevent your ads from displaying when certain keyword phrases are used, you can input negative keywords. Since I write books for nonfiction writers, I add "novel," "poetry," and "fiction" as negative keywords so Amazon doesn't serve up my ads when these words are in a search phrase.

Monitor Ad Performance

To know how your ads are performing, you can monitor the ad dashboard and drill down to see keyword performance. Here you will see the amount spent on ads and the amount earned in sales, which is represented in percentage format as the ACOS (average cost of sales). The lower this percentage, the more you are earning on your ads. Ideally you should aim for an ACOS rate of 70 percent or lower. You can easily turn off underperforming keywords.

It typically takes a day or two for your ad to be approved, and then a couple more days for your ad to start showing up in search results. Give any ads you set up at least sixty days to perform before you decide if they are worth the effort.

Here's an example of results from a brief ad I tested:

Budget	Impressions	Clicks	aCPC	Spend	Est. Total Sales	ACoS
Daily: $5	63,456	173	$0.16	$28.33	$163.85	17.29%

- In the above example, I set a daily budget of $5.
- The ad was displayed 63,456 times (Impressions) and received 173 clicks.
- The average cost per click was $0.16, for a total spend of $28.33 for the life of the ad.
- Total book sales generated totaled $163.85.
- If I subtract the cost of the ad ($28.33), my gross profit equaled $135.52. You do have to deduct the cost of printing if sales are based on print copies, as well as deduct Amazon's royalty from any Kindle sales, so these numbers are not exactly representative of profit.

Note that though my budget was $5 per day, because I only paid when the ad was clicked, the total dollars spent was far less than my daily budget. So, even if you set a daily budget, chances are that you may not end up spending that much. And if you do, ideally your ads will convert to enough book sales to make that spend worthwhile. And if you're seeing a solid ROI, increase your budget.

Ad Results by Keyword

When you click on your ad, you can drill down into results based on keywords. Here are some results for an ad for my book, *The Nonfiction Book Marketing Plan.*

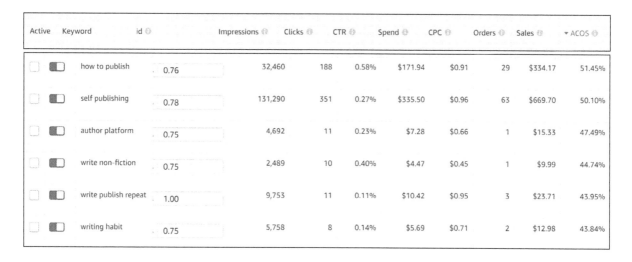

Active	Keyword	id	Impressions	Clicks	CTR	Spend	CPC	Orders	Sales	▾ ACOS
	how to publish	0.76	32,460	188	0.58%	$171.94	$0.91	29	$334.17	51.45%
	self publishing	0.78	131,290	351	0.27%	$335.50	$0.96	63	$669.70	50.10%
	author platform	0.75	4,692	11	0.23%	$7.28	$0.66	1	$15.33	47.49%
	write non-fiction	0.75	2,489	10	0.40%	$4.47	$0.45	1	$9.99	44.74%
	write publish repeat	1.00	9,753	11	0.11%	$10.42	$0.95	3	$23.71	43.95%
	writing habit	0.75	5,758	8	0.14%	$5.69	$0.71	2	$12.98	43.84%

I sorted the results based on the Average Cost of Sale (ACOS). The lower the percentage here, the better that keyword set is converting. At any time, you can log in to your Amazon advertising account and monitor your keywords or adjust those that aren't performing well.

When it comes to marketing, you never know what will perform best, which is why it's so important to spend time testing different strategies and choose lots of keywords for your ads.

PART 5

EXERCISE: Brainstorm Keyword Phrases for Ads

Remember to consider phrases your target reader might use to find your book, names of competing book titles, and competing authors. Open a separate browser so you can search Amazon to find keyword ideas.

Keywords	Keywords

PART 6

Prepare for Book Launch and Beyond

MOVE OUT OF YOUR COMFORT ZONE.
YOU CAN ONLY GROW
IF YOU ARE WILLING
TO FEEL AWKWARD
AND UNCOMFORTABLE
WHEN YOU TRY
SOMETHING NEW.

Brian Tracy

CHAPTER 17

Launch that Book

I f you've been reading each chapter of this book thoroughly, you might be fairly overwhelmed by now. Believe me, I understand how much work is involved in launching a book and how daunting it can be for new and experienced authors alike. However, this chapter takes you through the launch—the culmination of all the work you're doing. This is the fun part!

Before you pull the trigger on your book launch, there are some important details you should know about book distribution. Many authors would love to see their books on the shelves at brick-and-mortar stores. You can walk into your local Barnes and Noble and perhaps convince the manager to stock a few copies of your book because you're a local author, but that won't lead to national placement in retailers. Unfortunately, that's not how the system works. Most books are placed in stores by book distributors.

Understand Bookstore Distribution

Book distributors promote books to retailers. Some have a general focus to major stores like Barnes and Noble, while others sell to niches like schools, gift shops, Christian and metaphysical bookstores, and other specialty stores.

Many distributors won't work with just any book. You must apply and be accepted based on how well they anticipate your book selling. Factors include your book title and niche focus, cover design and overall book production quality, and the marketing plan you have behind your book. The distributor needs to be certain your book will sell before deciding to take it on.

Book distributors come with a price because they need to earn their fair piece of the pie. Brick-and-mortar stores take forty to fifty-five percent off the retail price, and distributors must pass along that discount. As a result, you can expect a distributor to take sixty-five to seventy-five percent off your retail price. These rates can make it difficult to achieve profitability.

For example, if your paperback is priced at $14.99, and a distributor takes seventy percent off that price, you would be paid $4.50 per copy. Then you need to deduct your print and shipping costs. If your book costs $3.25 to print and $.50 in landed shipping costs, your net profit would be $.75 per book.

Clearly, profit margins can be slim, unless you have a higher markup on your book and lower print costs. And there may be other expenses involved. You would likely be required to print, ship, and store hundreds or even thousands of books, which comes with a substantial investment before you even get started. Distributors sometimes charge an extra fee for storing books.

After you get past all these hurdles and a distributor is successful in placing your book in stores, then it's essential the book sells well. The key here is generating enough publicity and demand to drive shoppers to go out and buy your book from store shelves. Otherwise, you can find yourself having to accept huge quantities of returns.

The bookstore industry operates based on returns. If a book doesn't sell well within one to three months, it will be pulled from all store shelves and returned, with the expectation of a full refund. There are simply too many titles competing for shelf space. Returned books are often tossed carelessly into shipping boxes and damaged. But you still must issue the refund. And often you will be stuck with inventory that is too damaged to sell.

I don't know of another industry that operates like this. If Nordstrom doesn't sell out of a line of shirts, they don't get to return them to Michael Kors. They sell off the unsold items at a loss to TJ Maxx or Marshall's. Unfortunately, the bookstore industry doesn't work this way.

While seeing your book on bookstore shelves can bring a sense of accomplishment, it is not a true marker of success. The reality is that most book sales today happen online. Sadly, brick-and-mortar bookstores don't matter as much as they used to. And they can be one of the hardest places to sell books.

The one advantage that a bookstore brings to the table is that sales are reported to the *New York Times* Best Sellers lists. But it takes a tremendous number of sales—thousands of copies in a single week from brick-and-mortar stores across the country—to generate enough sales to make a dent in the list.

Create Reverse Demand with Bookstores

When you do the promotion work to build your author platform and create demand for your book, your readers will go looking for your book in their neighborhood bookstores. (Better yet, ask readers to go to their bookstores and request your book.) For self-published authors, most stores should be able to special order your books because you've set up distribution through Ingram. (Ingram distribution should be considered an essential step in your self-publishing journey.)

So, what do you think happens at Barnes and Noble when a manager notices they have special ordered a title several times? Or when the entire chain notices it's been special ordering books by the dozen—books that it doesn't yet stock? Yes, they come to you.

Barnes and Noble and other bookstores are operating a business, and they follow the money. If a book sells well, they order more. They have been known to contact authors directly about buying large quantities of books. Never forget that they follow the money.

They will prefer to purchase your books from Ingram (or another book distributor), so if you've made your book available at a discount of at least forty percent off the retail price, they will order your books. And they will potentially buy them in larger quantities if you are set up to accept returns. (I don't typically recommend accepting returns, though, unless you have a large platform and tremendous confidence that sales will happen.)

If you're interested in investigating book distributors, you can access a list of them here: nonfictionauthorsassociation.com/list-of-book-distributors-and-wholesalers/.

Reach the Best Sellers Lists

Getting featured on the *New York Times* Best Sellers list is a top goal for many authors, but unfortunately not an easy one to accomplish, especially when self-published. The coveted list is compiled each week based on sales in certain brick-and-mortar bookstores plus *some* online book sales.

The *New York Times* acknowledges that its list is curated based on stores it selects and not based on total units sold. This means that even though a book might sell 5,000 to 10,000 copies in a week (the average number of sales needed to appear on the list), if the newspaper doesn't deem the title worthy of its list, it won't appear. Unfortunately, this has happened to several self-published titles, which demonstrates what some view as a rather elitist approach by the paper.

One way self-published authors could previously circumvent the best sellers list requirements was to focus on e-book sales. However, in 2017 the *New York Times* removed several categories from its lists, including nonfiction e-books (as well as fiction e-books, young adult books, mass-market paperbacks, and several other categories). This is unfortunate, since we had previously celebrated as many self-published authors reached *New York Times* best seller status with e-book sales.

Unfortunately, the outlook for self-published authors who want to reach the *New York Times* list is bleak without exceptional brick-and-mortar bookstore distribution, a hefty promotion plan, and perhaps a starring role on a reality TV show. (*Survivor* or *Real Housewives*, anyone?)

With that said, the following details some other best sellers lists and what it takes to get there. You also never know when the rules might change, so let's hope that the stigma for self-published books continues to improve.

Wall Street Journal (WSJ)

While not as prestigious as the *New York Times*, the WSJ best sellers list is easier to reach because it's tabulated based on total units sold across all retailers, as reported by Nielsen BookScan (the industry standard in tracking book sales calculations). If you want your book to reach the WSJ list, especially if you've authored a business book, aim to sell 3,000 to 5,000 copies in a week. (Yes, it's daunting, but it's the reality.)

One way to boost your sales for the first week is to hold an Amazon presale for your book, beginning several weeks in advance. Any sales racked up will count on the official launch day. You can run Amazon ads while in presale and put all of your best marketing efforts in motion to drive those sales.

Note that sales must be acquired one book at a time. Bulk sales do not count, so ordering hundreds or even thousands of copies of your own book won't work. A better bet is to enlist thousands of family members, friends, clients, and social media followers to purchase copies of your book, one or two copies at a time.

USA Today

This list used to be compiled similar to the WSJ list, based on total book sales in print and digital formats combined. But today it's a curated list, much like the *New York Times*. Even worse, categories aren't listed so total sales fall under one primary list.

Publishers Weekly

This is more of an insider list for the publishing industry, but like the WSJ list, it's compiled based on total book sales as reported by Nielsen BookScan. The upside of this list is that publishing industry professionals, including literary agents, editors from major publishing houses, and librarians pay close attention to this list. They are always on the lookout for promising self-published authors, so if your book makes it onto this list, you could end up on the radar of some important publishing industry professionals.

Get Ready with Book Launch Incentives

I love giving incentives for book buyers during a book launch. Incentives help create urgency so that potential buyers go from thinking "I'll order it later when I have more time" (and then forgetting about it) to thinking "I need to buy this now!"

A book launch promotion can offer a variety of incentives for book buyers. The key is that the incentives have a perceived value and cannot easily be acquired anywhere else. You should treat this like a "free prize with purchase," not a contest. Contests have all kinds of regulations and in most states you cannot require a purchase to enter.

Incentives for book purchases could include any of the following, typically delivered as digital downloads:

- Companion worksheets or workbook
- Video training course
- Special report or bundle of reports
- Recipe book
- List of resources
- Templates or preformatted spreadsheets
- Bonus chapter
- Copy of your previous book
- Access to a private webinar you give on a future date
- Access to a course you offered in the past or will be offering soon

- Audio recordings
- Something that you normally sell but give for free with book purchase like a companion workbook

In order to host a promotion during your book launch, you will need to set up a registration form that automatically delivers the buyer's prize after registration is completed. Typically, the form includes a field for buyers to input an Amazon order number. You will have no way to verify order numbers, but in my experience, most people don't try to game the system. And if someone wants access to your free download even though he hasn't purchased the book, you haven't really lost much. You may instead gain a new fan as a result.

One of the smartest launch campaigns I've seen was when Colette Baron-Reid's book *The Map* was released. In lieu of incentives, buyers could enter to win dozens of prizes offered by her fellow authors at Hay House publishing. There was an elaborate website set up where you could click on each contributor's link, which would add you to their mailing list and enter you to win a prize. Prizes ranged from tickets to a cruise to consulting sessions with the promotion partners.

I liked that this campaign was out of the box and benefited all who participated. Baron-Reid's promotion partners benefited from lots of exposure and grew their mailing lists. Participants had a chance to win prizes, so it was treated like a contest. Note that in order to comply with contest regulations, a purchase was not required to enter. The promotion ran for several weeks and appeared to generate a ton of buzz.

The point is to get creative with your launch strategy and make it a win-win for you and your readers.

In more good news, you don't have to create all the bonus content yourself. David Newman, author of *Do It! Speaking: 77 Instant-Action Ideas to Market, Monetize, and Maximize Your Expertise* always offers bonuses with the purchase of his books. He creates a few special downloads of his own, and then reaches out to industry friends and asks them to contribute their own digital products.

Why would others contribute a bonus for David's launch? Because they know it will bring them exposure with his audience. I have gladly shared bonus content for his last two book launches. Reaching out to his industry peers and friends also gives David a reason to ask for their support on launch day and beyond, which has propelled his book sales in dramatic ways.

David doesn't just limit the bonuses to one day or one week. He keeps them listed on his book's sales page indefinitely. Many authors will offer buyer incentives on launch day, but I recommend spreading that out. At a minimum, offer incentives for a few weeks. Keeping your book launch campaign cranking gives you a fantastic reason to stay in contact with your audience and give them plenty of time to participate.

Note that if you decide to hold an incentive-based promotion, you will need to write this into all of your launch copy. It would be wise to have some graphics created as well so you can share visuals with your social media followers and email subscribers.

PART 6

Plan Your Launch Party

Planning a party to celebrate the release of your book, especially if it's your first book, can be a lot of fun. Publishing a book is a magnificent accomplishment and a lifelong dream for many. You deserve to celebrate that. There are many ways to approach a party. Authors can host parties at their homes, in bars or restaurants, and in unexpected venues like a home improvement store.

If you want your launch party to generate sales and build some buzz, then your best bet may be to hold it at a local bookstore. Most bookstores will gladly let you host your party there, even if you've self-published. Make sure you let the manager know that you plan to promote to friends and family and draw people into the store. As an added benefit, you can attract new buyers from those shopping in the store at the time.

Note that a launch party in a bookstore is different from a standard book-signing event. A launch party is a celebration where you invite people you know. A book-signing event is often just an author seated at a table in a store hoping to convince shoppers to buy a copy.

If you're a new or self-published author, most stores will likely offer to sell your books for you on consignment (you won't handle your own sales in a bookstore—they will want a piece of the action). The typical bookstore discount is forty to fifty-five percent, which means the store takes forty to fifty-five percent off of your retail price and pays you the remainder. For large chain stores, your check will be issued thirty to sixty days later, and they might ask to keep a few copies on display after the party ends.

If you're going to host a public launch party, pay attention to the details. Bring in items to decorate a display table. The store will likely provide a bare table for you so a tablecloth can be a good investment. Bring along your marketing collateral—bookmarks, postcards, etc. Also, make sure you have a way to get people to sign up for your email list. A simple basket or bowl for collecting business cards will do as long as you have a sign that offers some incentive in the form of a bonus download or a drawing for a free prize. You might serve cake, cupcakes, appetizers, or a simple bowl of candy. Balloons and signage can help draw attention too.

Ask the store staff to help you promote the release in advance. One way you can make it easy for them is to offer to print bag stuffers, which is just a simple flyer announcing the book launch event. You can have four of them cut out of each 8.5x11 sheet of paper and provide them to the store a couple weeks in advance. The store will want them to look very professional, so be sure to include the store logo and get their approval before you proceed with printing. You can also provide small posters for the store to display in advance if they are willing to do so.

At the launch party, plan something that will engage the crowd. You could give a reading from your book or a presentation. Better yet, give a brief talk at the top of each hour. Your party should last three or four hours so you can repeat your efforts. To add to the fun and encourage email list sign-ups, you might hold drawings throughout the event where you give away prizes.

Bob Quinlan, author of *Earn It: Empower Yourself for Love*, went all out for his launch party. He held the event at a local chain bookstore and hired a band to play outside in the front of the store on a beautiful summer afternoon. The store was located in a busy strip mall, so the band drew a crowd all by itself. Next to the band was a table hosted by Bob's friends, where visitors could sign up for the mailing list and enter to win raffle prizes. He collected generously donated prizes from local businesses prior to the event.

Inside, in the middle of the store, Bob had a projector and screen, several dozen chairs set up for an audience, and a display table where he signed books. He gave several brief talks throughout the afternoon covering tips from his book. In the end, he sold over one hundred books, and the store manager was so impressed that he kept Bob's books on display in some prime store real estate for several months after the event was over.

Most important to a successful launch party is that you start by inviting your friends and family. When you build your crowd, others will follow. They will want to know what all the fuss is about. Invite them to join you and don't forget to take lots of pictures of you in action, signing your books, and enjoying the crowd. Those will make impressive shots to share on your website and social media.

Host an Online Launch Party

The historic pandemic we've all experienced has driven many events to move online, which is one positive outcome of such a challenging time in our history. You can reach far more people online than you can in your own backyard—and no masks required!

If you decide to host a launch party online, you can make it fun. You could go live on Facebook, LinkedIn, or YouTube—or all of them throughout the day. You can engage your audience, create fun games or giveaways, and inspire participants to share across their own social media platforms. Remember, consumers listen to recommendations for books, restaurants, and just about anything. When others help spread the word about your book, those recommendations can go a long way.

EXERCISE: Send Launch Day Announcements—Checklist

Use these checklists to ensure you complete all essential launch tasks.
Send announcements to the following:

- ☐ Your email subscribers. Send a follow-up later in the day to report the progress and share screenshots showing your book in the top of categories.
- ☐ Everyone you identified in your Tribe of Influence, including peers, clients, coworkers, fellow authors, etc.
- ☐ Family and friends.
- ☐ Beta readers.
- ☐ Bloggers and podcasters from the research you did previously.
- ☐ Local and national media contacts.
- ☐ Trade association contacts, alumni groups, etc.
- ☐ Online groups that you belong to or manage.

☐ In-person groups that you're involved with. (Trade groups, chambers of commerce, Meetup.com, etc.)

☐ Anyone who provided an endorsement or is mentioned in your book.

EXERCISE: Share Social Media Content—Checklist

☐ Announce to social media groups that reach your target audience. (You may need to get permission from the group leader first.)

☐ Post the pre-written social media announcements you previously prepared.

☐ Share memes, infographics, and other images you prepared.

☐ Share screenshots of your book's progress with your social media audience and repeat posts throughout the day to keep the momentum building.

☐ Host a Facebook Live video event to engage your audience and build excitement.

☐ Host a LinkedIn Live video session.

☐ Add a video to YouTube and then invest in ads to promote it to your ideal audience.

☐ Repeat your Facebook and LinkedIn Live videos later in the day to report on progress.

☐ Monitor comments, direct messages, and mentions on social media so you can thank supporters, re-tweet their messages, and keep your audience engaged.

☐ Other:

EXERCISE: Monitor Launch Results—Checklist

☐ Monitor and track your book's sales rank on Amazon by taking screenshots every two hours.

☐ The lower the ranking, the more books you are selling.

☐ Monitor and track your book's position in its designated categories. Note that when you click on a category, you will see a section for "New Releases" in the category where your book may also be listed. Take screenshots to track your progress for each edition of your book (paperback, Kindle, hardcover, audiobook).

☐ Check email frequently to monitor feedback from your audience and address any issues or questions that may arise.

☐ Share screenshots with your social media followers.

☐ Share screenshots with your email subscribers later in the day to let them know their support is helping.

☐ Send thank-you messages to those who buy the book or help spread the word.

☐ Other:

CHAPTER 18

Become a Professional Speaker

Break into Professional Speaking

If there is one thing I know for sure, it's this: Speakers sell books. Speaking is one of the best ways to grow your audience and generate book sales because you can connect with large groups of people. As a speaker, you demonstrate your authority in your subject matter. When you educate and entertain an audience, attendees will want to take a piece of you home with them—which means they will buy your books and other products and services you offer.

To get started, you can give free talks to local organizations and work your way up to paid speaking gigs, if paid speaking is a priority for you. You can keep yourself quite busy doing free speeches within a 100-mile radius of where you live. Free presentations can have many advantages because you gain exposure with the organization's entire network, not just the people who attend your session, and you can sell books at the back of the room.

Choose Compelling Speaking Topics

When it comes to choosing topics for your speaking engagements, remember that it's not about you or your book; it's about your audience. Your topics should provide value for attendees. What will they learn? How will their lives improve because of your presentation? These are questions to consider as you develop topics.

For prescriptive nonfiction authors, the task of developing speaking topics should be relatively easy since they often relate to the content in your book. For memoir and narrative nonfiction authors, you may need to get creative. If you've authored a memoir about overcoming an illness, you might create a motivational presentation about how to persevere in tough times—this will make it more relatable to a wide variety of audiences. For an author of a historical work, you could speak about the process you used to do your research or share historical facts related to your book.

Speakers often have several presentation topics available in order to offer a variety of choices to event organizers. Just be sure topics are aligned with each other. It could confuse your audience if you have topics ranging from how to get organized to strategies for managing mental health.

Write a Compelling Description

You will need a brief and interesting description for each presentation, including three to five bullet points explaining the benefits for the audience. The description of your presentation is an important tool in helping you get booked for engagements, so be sure it demonstrates how your content meets the needs of the audience.

Not only is your presentation description used by decision makers, but it will also get copied and pasted into event programs and marketing materials prior to your event and posted online. Therefore, your event hosts want to see a compelling description that can excite their potential attendees.

Ideally, you should choose at least one signature presentation topic. This is the main presentation you can deliver to just about any audience. Additional topics can also help you get booked. Be creative with presentation titles and angles so that you stand out against competitors.

Develop a Speaker One-Sheet

Most professional speakers have a one- or two-page flier that they can give to potential event hosts to promote their speaking topics. Often, event planners gather in a room with a stack of speaker sheets when deciding what speakers to invite to their conference or event, so this is an important piece of marketing collateral.

Your sheet should include a brief overview of one or more speaking topics, testimonials from past presentations if you have them, a list of past audiences if available, your photo, book cover, and contact information.

Add a Speaker Page to Your Website

Take the information from your speaker sheet and add it to a page on your website. You may be surprised to discover how this effort alone can attract opportunities to speak.

EXERCISE: Develop Your Speaker Content

- ☐ Write a captivating title and description for your signature presentation.
- ☐ Write titles and descriptions for two additional presentations.
- ☐ Create a speaker one-sheet.
- ☐ Add a speaker page to your website.
- ☐ Round up endorsements from previous audiences, if available.
- ☐ If you have access to any video of you speaking, add it to your speaker page. If you have several videos recorded, considering hiring a video editor to create a speaker trailer. Video is especially important if you're aiming to get paid speaking engagements.

EXERCISE: Write Your Speaker Pitch

Craft a letter you can send by email to pitch yourself as a speaker to organizations.

Sample Speaker Pitch

Your email pitch should be quick and to the point. Here's an example:

> Greetings <name>,
>
> I'm an author and speaker specializing in healthy lifestyle habits for employees in the workforce and I'm reaching out to inquire about speaking to <group/organization name>.
>
> Here are some potential topics I can cover:
>
> - Topic one
> - Topic two
> - Topic three
>
> My goal is to inspire audiences to want to make small changes that lead to living longer, fuller, happier lives. I know you have a lot of technology professionals in your group, and they typically work long hours. They are an ideal audience for these presentations and will find the content quite valuable.
>
> I have attached my speaker sheet, and you can also learn more about me on my website:
>
> <link to speaker page on your site>
>
> Can we schedule time for a brief chat?
>
> Thank you,
>
> Suzy Speaker

Pro Tip: Ending a pitch with a question helps inspire a reply, even if it's just to say no thank you. And it's a powerful way to get event organizers on the phone so you can learn about their audience and event and discuss the opportunities, rather than going back and forth by email.

PART 6

Locate Speaking Opportunities

Following are many ways to locate speaking engagement opportunities.

Trade Associations

There are thousands of associations that hold monthly meetings and annual conferences. You are more likely to get paid for larger events, but local events need speakers too, especially for chapters that hold monthly meetings. Here are some directories to locate associations:

- DirectoryofAssociations.com.
- National Trade and Professional Associations Directory – This is a large-sized printed book that starts at around $350 to purchase and $800 for access to an online directory. You can often find a copy at your local library or you can purchase a used copy on Amazon or eBay. Or purchase a copy here: associationexecs.com/national-trade-and-professional-associations-directory.
- Marketing Mentor – Maintains a smaller list of associations. Categories include business, healthcare, law/legal, and more: marketing-mentor.com/pages/trade-list.
- You can locate many association meetings in your own backyard with some simple Google searches. Example: <your city> + "association." This could be "Sacramento association" or "Orlando association."

Conferences and Trade Shows

Look for events that reach your target audience and then search for their speaker submission guidelines. You may need to reach out to event organizers or other staff to inquire about opportunities. Here are some event directories:

- 10times.com/events
- eventsinamerica.com
- eventseye.com
- orbus.com/about-us/usa-tradeshow-list

Corporate Events

Big money can be found by speaking at corporate events. Finding these can take some effort, though. Here are some ways to do so:

- Search Google for <industry> + "conference." Example: "women's health conference" or "technology conference." Note that you may need to build a list and keep track for the following year since speakers are often planned many months in advance.

- Meeting Professionals International is the top association for meeting planners. They often host showcases for speakers where event planners can see speakers in action with the goal of potentially inviting speakers to their future events: mpiweb.org.

Nonprofits and Charities

Just as trade associations host monthly and annual meetings, so do nonprofits. And many of the larger nonprofits are well-funded and pay speakers, even for speaking at monthly chapter meetings.

- IRS Directory of Nonprofits is compiled by our friends at the IRS:
- irs.gov/charities-non-profits/charities-non-profits-a-z-site-index.
- Love to Know lists several dozen popular nonprofits: charity.lovetoknow.com/List_of_Nonprofit_Organizations.
- Candid offers a handy search feature: candid.org/.

Industry Publications

Read trade magazines, newsletters, and blogs for event announcements.

Local Service Organizations

Groups like Rotary, Kiwanis, and Optimist Club welcome speakers, often on a weekly basis. They also appreciate a wide variety of topics. Contact chapters in your area to inquire about opportunities to speak at their frequently held meetings.

Chambers of Commerce

Nearly every city has a chamber organization, and these groups love to welcome speakers. You won't likely get paid, but you'll have an opportunity to connect with your local community, and that can often lead to subsequent opportunities.

Colleges

Schools of all sizes welcome speakers and often pay them.

- For colleges, start with the campus activities coordinator for the school you want to target. You can also contact individual department heads, such as the History Department or Women's Studies. Don't be afraid to get creative. Locating one good contact can help you get connected to another simply by asking.
- The National Association for Campus Activities (naca.org) and the Association for Promotion of Campus Activities (apca.com) both hold showcase events for speakers and entertainers.

PART 6

Grade, Middle, and High Schools

For grade, middle, and high schools, contact school administrators and send a pitch. Hint: if you can turn your event into a school fundraiser by offering the school a percentage of book sales, you may have better luck getting your foot in the door.

Houses of Worship

Religious institutions of all kinds welcome speakers with something to offer their congregation. For example, the Unity Church is known for being author-friendly and will gladly host special events. You can potentially tour their locations across the nation.

Libraries

Almost all libraries welcome speakers, especially authors who are speakers. You won't get paid, but make sure you're allowed to sell books. Start with your local library and collect testimonials as you go.

Bookstores

While many stores host authors for book-signing events, you can sell far more books when you show up as a speaker and give the audience valuable information.

Local Event Directories

You can keep yourself busy speaking to Meetup.com groups in your area and beyond. Also search Eventbrite.com and Facebook Events to mine for opportunities, both in-person and online.

Speakers Bureaus

Speakers bureaus connect top keynote speakers with large events, and they take a percentage of the speaking fee (typically twenty-five percent to thirty percent). Celebrities get the most action from bureaus because they earn top dollar and are easiest to place at events. However, if you have a niche topic and a lot of experience, plus some edited video of you presenting, it may be worthwhile to pursue getting listed with one or more speakers bureaus. A quick Google search will show you many options. Follow each bureau's guidelines to submit your materials for consideration. See also the International Association of Speakers Bureaus, which offers a searchable directory to locate bureaus by state: iasbweb.org/.

Specific Industries

Consider pitching yourself as a speaker to any of the following:

- First responders' departments (police, fire)
- Retirement communities
- Real estate offices
- Financial planning firms
- Corporations for "lunch and learn" sessions
- Retailers
- Shopping malls (they NEED events to bring in people)
- Casinos
- Car dealerships
- Restaurants
- Media offices (like your local newspaper)
- Adult learning centers
- Parks and recreation departments
- Military organizations
- Hospitals and healthcare centers

As you can see, there are endless options for locating speaking opportunities. This is one of the top ways authors sell books. While the pandemic has altered the state of in-person events, it's prompted many events to move online. I view this as a positive change because you can potentially reach even more people without stepping outside your front door.

EXERCISE: Connect with Associations, Groups, and Nonprofits

There are a variety of ways you can work with trade associations, nonprofits, and other professional groups. Following are some opportunities to consider. Check all that you're interested in pursuing.

- ☐ Speak at their weekly or monthly meetings.
- ☐ Speak at their conferences.
- ☐ Tour their chapters as a speaker.
- ☐ Contribute articles to their blog, newsletter, or magazine.
- ☐ Be a guest on their podcast.
- ☐ Join the board of directors or volunteer so you can become known as a leader.
- ☐ Host a fundraiser and split the revenue from your book sales.
- ☐ Ask them to purchase a large quantity of your books to give away to new members or distribute at their events.

- ☐ Sell them a license to digital copies of your book to distribute to members.
- ☐ Ask them to sell your book in their bookstore.
- ☐ Propose delivering educational workshops or events for their members.

If you plan to reach out to associations, nonprofits, local groups, online groups, or any other major organization, your pitch can make or break the results, so it's important that you put a lot of care into crafting your letter. Whenever you make any kind of sales pitch, the most important question to ask yourself is this: *What's in it for the recipient?*

The key here is to highlight the benefits for the organization and give them an offer they can't pass up. Here's an example:

> Dear Polly President,
>
> I've been a member of The Gluten Allergy and Sensitivity Alliance for many years, and it's an organization I am proud to support. Since my son and I both live with severe gluten sensitivity, I wanted to let you know about my new book, which will be out this spring: *Avoiding Gluten on the Go: How to Ensure Food Safety when Traveling.*
>
> I am certain that every member of GASA could benefit from this book because it can prevent the frustration and danger of dining out while traveling. I have enclosed a copy of the book for you to personally review.
>
> Would you consider offering a copy of *Avoiding Gluten* to new members who join GASA, and adding it to the online resources section for existing members? I would be happy to offer a bulk discount rate on a purchase of one hundred or more copies.
>
> I hope you find the book useful in your own travels. Could we schedule time for a quick call to discuss in greater detail?
>
> Thank you kindly for your consideration,
>
> Annie Author

By the way, you can mail a printed letter with a copy of your book or you can send it by email with a link to access a digital copy of the book.

EXERCISE: Write Your Pitch to Associations

- ☐ Address the recipient by name, when possible.
- ☐ Create a personal connection by sharing your membership status or involvement in the group.
- ☐ Detail your pitch and its benefits for the organization.

- ☐ If you have multiple pitch ideas, list them briefly but beware of overwhelming your recipient. Plant just a few seeds to get a conversation going.
- ☐ End with a question, such as, "Can we schedule time for a brief phone call?" Ending with a question can prompt a quick response from the recipient.
- ☐ Include your contact information, a link to book details, or any other information you feel would be relevant or helpful.

Host Webinars and Online Events

There are countless benefits to hosting online events, which can bring people together without the need for travel—saving time and money for all involved. Webinars are the most common type of online event, and they can be used for a variety of purposes.

Promotional (Free) Webinars

One powerful way to leverage webinars is to offer these events for free in exchange for capturing email addresses from attendees. Many businesses and online marketers promote educational webinars to introduce audiences to new topics and then ultimately entice them into an "upsell" for related products and services. Free webinars can be a valuable marketing tool for reaching potential readers and customers around the globe to build your email list, promote your book, or promote other products and services.

Complimentary webinars can also be hosted by organizations that simply want to offer valuable content to their members or the community at large. I serve on the board of a nonprofit that hosts free monthly webinars featuring guest speakers aimed at providing support to members of the organization. There is no upsell involved; these events are delivered as a service to the community. (And by the way, the speakers are often authors looking to mention their books.)

You can host your own webinars and promote them to your email list and social media followers. You can also offer complimentary webinars through places of worship, all kinds of businesses, service organizations, groups, nonprofits, and more. Webinars are inexpensive to host and are easier than ever to deliver with tools like Zoom.

Paid Webinars

Another way to leverage webinar technology is to charge attendees for participation. All kinds of organizations, from private businesses to nonprofits, offer educational webinars. These often feature guest instructors and charge fees ranging from $10 to $50 to attend a short event. Webinar events can also be recorded for later viewing or sold as a bundled offering.

PART 6

Online Courses

A series of webinar events can also be compiled and delivered as part of an online course. For example, you could offer a four-part course delivered each week with ninety-minute instructional webinar events. These live events can allow attendees to interact with the host and each other, get questions answered, and feel they are part of the program.

Online Conferences

When the pandemic hit in 2020, organizations of all sizes had to figure out how to transform their in-person conferences into online events. Thankfully, I've been hosting the Nonfiction Writers Conference (NFWC) entirely online since 2010, so the various stay-at-home orders affecting most of us didn't hurt our event at all. In fact, attendance has since been higher than ever.

My personal mission has always been to make NFWC as valuable as an in-person event, while saving attendees time and travel costs. Our events attract participants and speakers from around the globe.

Long before the pandemic, I wondered why so many associations and companies were ignoring the opportunity to host conferences online. While I won't claim it's easy to host a large online event, it certainly has far less financial risk than renting a hotel, ordering catering, flying in and housing speakers and staff, and managing the countless other details that go into hosting events for large groups of people.

For NFWC, we use Zoom to broadcast live presentations over three days. Attendees can opt to participate in our live pitch session with literary agents, which is wildly popular. We even offer one-on-one consultations between attendees and industry experts who share advice in fifteen-minute sessions by phone or video chat. A private Facebook group is available to all participants, making networking far less intimidating than it can be at an in-person event.

If your industry could benefit from an online conference, I urge you to consider creating one. To get started, you will need some compelling speakers, a Zoom webinar account, ecommerce to collect payments, and enthusiasm for bringing people together.

If you want to learn more about how to break into professional speaking, check out our course created exclusively for authors.

https://nonfictionauthorsassociation.com/professional-speaking-course-for-authors/

EXERCISE: Plan Your Online Events

Answer the following questions:

What types of events would you like to host? (Webinars, courses, or conferences.)

_____

_____

_____

_____

What will the duration be for your event(s)?

_____

_____

_____

_____

What topics will you cover?

_____

_____

_____

_____

When can you schedule your first event?

_____

_____

_____

_____

What steps do you need to take to prepare for your event?

_____

_____

_____

_____

PART 6

CHAPTER 19

Keep the Marketing Momentum Going

Marketing doesn't stop when the book is released. In fact, you're just getting started. Use the momentum from your launch to propel you forward. Long-term success requires ongoing effort, whether we're talking about book sales, weight loss, or learning to play an instrument. Big rewards require big effort.

Following are some of my favorite ways to keep building your influence and selling books.

Generate Bulk Book Sales

Selling your books in bulk can be lucrative. It can also eliminate the headaches that come from distributing books via the typical bookstore model, since bookstores expect to be able to return unsold books. Corporations and specialty stores do not expect you to accept returns.

There are plenty of places to sell your books in large quantities. Here are some to consider:

- Corporations can distribute your books at their events or tradeshows. Instead of a coffee mug, pen, or other boring promotional item, they can give away your books.
- Companies can distribute books to their customers or employees. When the book *Who Moved My Cheese?* by Spencer Johnson, Kenneth Blanchard, et al. gained popularity, companies all over the US bought thousands of copies to distribute to employees with the goal of helping them embrace change (often in the form of downsizing, unfortunately).
- Nonprofit organizations can distribute books to members or at their events.
- You could find a corporate sponsor to donate copies of your book to a nonprofit.
- You can work with companies and nonprofits to create a custom version of your book. Print their logo on the cover and allow them to insert a custom introduction, special chapter, or even an advertisement.
- Retailers could give away your books as a bonus with purchase. For example, if you wrote a book on wellness with vitamins, convince your local drugstore or health food store to feature your book near the supplements section.

PART 6

- Specialty retailers like gift shops, car washes, gas stations, etc. can stock your books for sale or give it away as a bonus with purchase.
- A local business might be thrilled to set up a large display of your books to entice new customers. For example, a bank could give your business book away to new banking customers. After the promotion is successful in a local branch, ask to speak to someone at corporate headquarters who could approve the promotion across all branches.
- Consider service-based businesses like insurance agencies, travel agents, mortgage and real estate companies, and day spas. Could your book benefit their customers?

Think big and you could generate some tremendous bulk sales as a result.

EXERCISE: Brainstorm Bulk Sales Opportunities

What kinds of retailers would make a good match for your book? (Who reaches your target audience?)

_____

_____

_____

_____

_____

_____

_____

_____

_____

What companies could benefit from giving your books away to employees or customers?

_____

_____

_____

_____

_____

_____

_____

_____

_____

_____

What nonprofits would be a good match for your book?

_____

_____

_____

_____

_____

_____

_____

_____

Where do your book buyers shop or conduct business?

_____

_____

_____

_____

_____

_____

_____

_____

_____

What causes are important to your target audience?

_____

_____

_____

_____

_____

_____

_____

_____

_____

PART 6

Promote Your Book to Colleges

One of the many benefits of writing nonfiction is that we can educate our readers. Whether we do that with a how-to guide, a memoir, history, science, or other kind of reference book, many well-written nonfiction books have the potential to be adopted into curriculum for college courses.

Getting colleges to adopt my books as part of the curriculum wasn't something I ever planned on, but when I was contacted by a professor who wanted to use my first book (a business start-up guide) in his course, I was thrilled. It was even more exciting to realize that at least fifty copies of my book would be reordered each semester just for that one class—and that sales could be replicated each time my book was adopted for another college course.

After agreeing to ship the required books directly to the college bookstore and cutting out the distributor, the professor asked if I'd be willing to deliver a Skype interview during class time and answer questions from the students. I gladly accepted, and we scheduled the appearance toward the end of the semester. The students were eager to speak to me as the author and asked compelling questions that were fun to answer. Since then, I've had several arrangements like this for various books I've written. And you can, too.

How to Locate Key Contacts at Schools

The course instructors and professors decide what books to use in their curriculum, which means you need to identify who they are and determine how to reach them. This requires some research.

You will want to seek out professors who teach the courses that align with your book. For example, if you've authored a book about career options for human resources professionals, then you'll want to find instructors who teach HR-related courses. If you've authored a memoir on your experience in combat, you'll want to find instructors covering military history.

You can begin by searching school faculty directories, which are almost always available online. Another way to locate names and contact information is through LinkedIn. Many course instructors maintain up-to-date profiles on LinkedIn.

A search on LinkedIn for "marketing professor" returns over 500,000 results. You may need to narrow down your search by city, state, or specific college.

How to Contact Course Instructors

Once you locate a name, you have several options:

- You can mail a review copy of your book, along with a personal note.
- You can mail a postcard asking if the instructor would like to receive a review copy, along with instructions for contacting you.
- You can send an email asking if the instructor would like a review copy.

Regardless of how you reach out, you're going to have to let them evaluate the book, which means sending out complimentary review copies.

How to Handle Book Sales to Colleges

Traditionally, colleges want their on-site bookstore to manage book sales. This means the store may want to order from a distributor like Ingram. They will always expect a discount, and that can range from thirty to fifty percent off the retail price. Some may be willing to order directly from you as the author.

And because schools are evolving with the times, the instructor may even suggest her students buy the book on Amazon or another online retailer. She may want it to be available in e-book and print formats. Be prepared for all kinds of scenarios.

Additional Tips for Success

Once you land your first college, you can mention that in your pitches to other schools, which only helps to build on your credibility. Also, let each instructor know that you are willing to assist through a Zoom or Skype interview with students or with study guides or other materials. Make it easy for them to say yes!

If getting your books placed in colleges becomes a top focus for you, you might consider creating a special textbook edition of your book. It could include some compelling questions, a study guide, or be printed in full color. It can also be priced higher than a typical book since the textbook market has always been notoriously expensive.

Getting your books adopted by colleges can become an excellent recurring sales channel. But perhaps even more importantly, it can be incredibly rewarding on a personal level. When your book makes an impact on readers in such a powerful way, all that hard work you did to write, publish, and market your book can prove to be worthwhile.

Consider Book Promotion Sites

Book promotion sites offer books for free or at a discount to eager readers. They build email lists based on readers' genre interests. Book giveaways and low-price promotions have a history of working well for fiction. These promotions can work to boost sales for nonfiction too, though certain categories may have a harder time finding an audience on these sites. For example, technology books and other niches may not perform as well.

These promotions are rather affordable, so it can be worth testing, especially if your book sales are lagging and you want to bring some new life into them. Here are some sites to investigate:

- Goodreads giveaways
- LibraryThing

- BookBub
- FreeBooksy
- BookRiot

Invest in Advertising

All kinds of products and services are sold through paid advertising, and books are no exception. However, because books typically have a low profit margin, it can be difficult to achieve a return on investment (ROI) from many forms of traditional and online advertising.

You may want to invest in advertising with bargain book sites like <u>BookBub.com</u> and <u>FreeBooksy.com</u>. The idea here is to enlist your ebook in free or low-cost promotions to gain readership. These programs can be effective for boosting sales to readers of fiction and some nonfiction; however, don't expect massive sales numbers. Due to discounting, you will do well to earn back your advertising investment. These bargain book sites are more about building buzz and acquiring book reviews. Another service that promotes books to readers and doesn't require you to deeply discount your book is <u>BookRiot.com</u>.

Ads on Google, Facebook, X, and LinkedIn can be tricky because the rates make it difficult to earn a profit from book sales alone. With that said, certain niche topics can perform well, provided you have a deep understanding of how these ad platforms work (or hire someone who does) and you are able to appeal to target readers. Technical manuals, highly specialized topics, and books with a higher price point can be successful at generating enough revenue to justify the ad expense with these types of ads.

There are also advertising opportunities in a wide variety of media outlets, though you should choose wisely. Top newspapers and magazines can charge more than $2,000 for a single inch of ad space. Even midsize publications can be pricey. The same goes for radio and television advertising. Unless you have a massive budget to produce your own infomercial or public broadcasting program, these outlets are likely out of reach.

However, there are all kinds of specialty publications to consider.

- Smaller magazines—and there are tons of them. Here are some titles that demonstrate an abundance of niche advertising opportunities: *Artists and Illustrators, Hobby Farms, Evolve, Brainspace, Digital Camera World, In-Fisherman, Chickens, Crochet World, Working Mother, Custom Car, Spirituality and Health, Mindset,* and *Model Railroader.*
- Regional magazines and newspapers in every city in the country (and around the world).
- Trade association newsletters, magazines, and blogs.
- Nonprofit newsletters, magazines, and blogs.
- Niche websites that feature banner ads and sponsored ads to their email subscribers.

Paid advertising can be challenging when it comes to ROI, and it rarely works as a stand-alone strategy. It's best to make advertising just one spoke in your marketing wheel.

Submit to Book Awards Programs

There are a good number of book awards programs where authors can compete to win an award. Most awards programs charge a fee for entry, and the guidelines typically allow for books published in the previous calendar year. Some programs are extra-friendly to independent authors, and there are other programs that don't even allow indie authors to participate. (They clearly haven't caught up with the times yet.)

Authors often ask me if it's worthwhile to participate in awards programs, and my answer is almost always yes. When your book receives an award, your title instantly changes from "author" to "award-winning author." Your book will likely get a slight publicity boost from the awards program itself, and you can get a lot of bragging rights.

Most programs will sell you stickers you can place on your books to promote your winning status, along with badges you can feature on your website. You can also update your book's sales pages and descriptions on online bookstores to acknowledge the award. Your award-winning author status can impress prospective readers and boost sales. And perhaps even more importantly, winning an award can bring a tremendous amount of personal satisfaction. It's a big accomplishment to write a book in the first place, and to have your work recognized can be so rewarding.

Following are some top book awards programs for independent authors.

Nonfiction Book Awards – Year-round program honoring the best in nonfiction. Books are independently evaluated, not judged against other titles. Full disclosure: This program is run by the Nonfiction Authors Association, the organization I founded in 2013.
nonfictionauthorsassociation.com/nonfiction-book-awards/

Ben Franklin Book Awards – Recognizing independently published books and hosted by IBPA.
ibpabenjaminfranklinaward.com/

Global E-Book Awards – The first awards program exclusively for e-books, hosted by self-publishing godfather Dan Poynter.
globalebookawards.com/

Foreword Indies Awards – Hosted by *Foreword* magazine, this is an indie-friendly awards program.
forewordreviews.com/awards/

Nautilus Book Awards – Recognizes books that promote spiritual growth, conscious living, and positive social change.
nautilusbookawards.com/

Buy Your Way to a Larger Author Platform

One of the most common questions I've heard from countless authors over the years is, "How do I just outsource my book marketing?" There is usually a tragic look of disappointment when I cite the many reasons why it's nearly impossible to outsource book marketing AND earn enough profit from sales to justify the cost. Books have tiny profit margins, which makes it hard to invest money in marketing and earn a return on investment (ROI).

But not all authors care about the bottom line.

Some authors are more interested in getting books in readers' hands regardless of what it costs. It is often because the book is a marketing tool for other business goals, like generating consulting clients or speaking opportunities, and therefore a larger marketing budget is justified because one new client can pay for a year of marketing expenses.

Whether you're just getting started with book marketing or you've been at it for a while, if you have a budget to spend and ROI isn't your primary focus, there are ways you can invest in building your audience. While some authors spend years working hard at building their platforms, even a small investment can go a long way in growing your platform and generating book sales.

Following are some of the many ways to build your platform and sell more books by investing in your author business.

Amazon Ads

Just about every author should try Amazon ads because when done correctly, these ads should pay for themselves. Ads are created through your KDP account for the Kindle edition of your book, though they can lead to sales of your print books too. For someone with an unlimited budget, you can dedicate ad dollars and ramp up your efforts in a big way. We covered this in great detail in chapter 16.

Facebook Page Ads

You can invest in ads to promote your Facebook page and attract page "likes" or fans. Remember, we're talking about investing budget to build your platform—and this strategy is not inexpensive. Page ads can help you build your fan base on Facebook, and then you can promote posts to those fans. Unfortunately, Facebook doesn't allow you to access contact information for your audience, so once you have some page followers, your next job is to entice your fans to join your email list.

Facebook Ads to Build Your Email List

One of my favorite tactics is to use Facebook ads to build my own email list, which is accomplished by promoting a downloadable report or similar freebie, or access to a webinar or other type of free event. This is content marketing at its best. Give your audience something of value in exchange for signing up for your email list.

Start by creating a registration page where you capture contact information, and then hop on over to Facebook advertising and promote the post. You can create all kinds of custom audiences on Facebook. You can target your ads towards fans of competing pages. You can upload lists of contacts and target your ads to those people. You can also let Facebook create a "look-alike" audience—people with similar interests—based on your contacts lists. I've found lookalike audiences to be quite effective. You can also target ads based on geographic location, hobbies and interests, job title, and much more.

You will pay per click for these ads, and prices can range from $.20 per click to over $3 for highly competitive audiences. Remember, you're aiming to drive registration to your mailing list, which you can then use to build your author business.

Social Media Ads

Facebook isn't the only platform for advertising. You can grow your following on any of the social media networks using targeted ads. Just make sure you have an end goal in mind. Do you want to drive subscribers to your email list? Do you want to build an audience with valuable content and then entice them to buy your books and other products? Make sure you're clear about your plan before you spend a dime.

- LinkedIn – These are typically the most expensive ads, though useful for those who want to reach a business audience. (Hint: professional speakers and executive-level service providers can expand your reach here.)
- X – They offer affordable auto-targeting and other advertising options.
- Instagram – Owned by Facebook, you can feed your Facebook ads directly into Instagram.
- Pinterest – An excellent platform if you cover home decorating, cooking, arts and crafts, fashion, or anything else targeted toward women.
- YouTube – Reach all kinds of audiences with content and ads here.

Surveys

SurveyMonkey is an inexpensive tool for building surveys, which you can use to learn more about your audience. The Nonfiction Authors Association uses surveys to assess how our conference attendees enjoyed our events. We also host an annual survey to learn more about the demographics of our members, what topics they want to learn about, and what member benefits are most valuable.

You can take surveys a step further and use them to build your email list. SurveyMonkey offers the ability to promote your surveys online with paid ads. To make this effective, your survey needs to do two things: attract your target audience and most importantly, collect their email addresses when they submit their responses. You can entice survey participants by holding a drawing for one or more prizes. The chance to win can entice participation. You can also turn your survey into a quiz, which can sound more appealing to users.

Review Copies

For an author with a budget to spend, sending out review copies can lead to all kinds of opportunities. As we discussed earlier, advanced review copies, also known as ARCs, were traditionally sent to media with the goal of generating book reviews. But it's not easy for indie authors to get traditional book reviews, and there are other ways you can benefit from sending out review copies.

For example, many consultants, coaches, attorneys, financial advisors, business brokers, and other professionals send out hundreds and even thousands of copies of their books to generate business leads. You can also mail out review copies to industry influencers who could potentially mention your book in their blogs, podcasts, videos, social media, or other venue. You'll need to do some research to build a list of influencers to send copies to, but this can lead to all kinds of publicity.

Airport Bookstore Placement

Getting books sold through airport bookstores is a goal for many authors. It's not easy, but it's also not impossible. You should know that premium placement in these stores is usually *purchased* by publishers and book distributors. That's right, the books you see prominently displayed on endcaps in airport bookstores are usually placed there based on advertising fees that cost as much as $5,000 per month.

Why would an author spend $5,000 to place a book on an endcap in airport stores? Many business books are used as high-end business cards for authors who offer consulting, sales training programs, and other high-dollar corporate programs. That investment can be earned back each time an executive buys the book and decides to hire the author's company.

Advertising placement fees aren't the only way to get into these stores. You can get your book considered for placement, though know that the standards are extremely high. Your book must have the highest production quality possible. It needs an exceptional cover and extensive editing.

You will also need to work with a book wholesaler to get your books considered for placement in airport bookstores or any brick-and-mortar store. We maintain a list of book distributors here: nonfictionauthorsassociation.com/list-of-book-distributors-and-wholesalers/.

Also consider pitching your book to gift shops at airports instead of the actual airport bookstores. Here are some of the top airport retailers:

- Hudson Booksellers: hudsonbooksellers.com/book-submissions (Note their website states they won't accept any books produced by KDP.)
- Paradies Lagardère: paradieslagardere.com
- WH Smith (UK-based): whsmith.co.uk

Hire a Virtual Assistant—Your Secret to Success

The reality is that no successful author does it all alone. One of my personal mottos is "the more I hire, the more I earn!" I strongly encourage you to hire help so you can focus on what you do best.

A virtual assistant (VA) is an independent contractor who typically works from home and supports several clients. VAs can help with administrative tasks, social media management, blog content, sending out pitches, conducting research, and much more. You can hire an assistant for as few as five hours per month to help with all the tasks you tend to neglect or don't have time for. Find an assistant who has experience working with authors.

We maintain a list of assistants here: AuthorsAssistantDirectory.com.
See also: TheVirtualSavvy.com, VANetworking.com, and Upwork.com.

Bonus Book Marketing Action Plan Template

If you'd like to track your book marketing tasks in a spreadsheet, we've preformatted one with multiple tabs to help you get organized. Download our free Book Marketing Action Plan template and other bonus items: http://workbookbonus.com.

Additional resources, including recommended service providers:
nonfictionauthorsassociation.com/recommended-resources

If you have knowledge,
let others
light their candles with it.

———

WINSTON CHURCHILL

CHAPTER 20

Bring Home the Bacon

I f you've made it through your book launch and completed most of the exercises in this workbook, take a moment to congratulate yourself. There is nothing easy about writing, publishing, and launching a book into the world. Being a successful author takes work and time and dedication. It's a level of commitment that not everyone can make.

If you've come this far and realized all this effort isn't for you, that's okay too. We all have different motivations and goals for our books. Maybe you just want your book to be read by some family members and friends. Or perhaps you have other priorities in life right now and this isn't the time for you to put in the amount of effort needed. Whatever your situation may be, you now have the tools so you can pick up where you left off when the time is right.

The reality is a large percentage of authors give up on book marketing, often within a couple months of their book launch. This means many of your competitors will fall off the map. Take a moment to peruse Amazon for competing books. How many titles have less than ten reviews? Those authors might be just getting started, but if the books have been out for a while, there is a good chance they don't know how to do the essential marketing work, or they have simply given up the race. This gives you a tremendous competitive advantage.

When you dedicate yourself to the processes involved in book marketing, when you're persistent and committed, your efforts will inevitably pay off. This is how life works.

Consider this: If you wanted to train to run a marathon, you would need to commit to running each day to meet your goal. You would carve out the time in your calendar and make it a priority. You would set milestones that you want to meet. Each week, your time and distance would improve and prepare you for the race.

Conversely, if you're a non-runner (like me!), you wouldn't decide to run a full marathon in thirty days. It's not logical or reasonable. (Neither is launching a book in thirty days with absolutely no audience or marketing plan.) You must create a reasonable timeline, set a plan, and then consistently make progress in order to reach your marathon goal.

Nearly every kind of success in life is cumulative. Accomplishment comes from small steps made on a consistent basis that add up over time and enable you to reach your goals.

- If you want to become a better guitar player, you must schedule time to practice several days each week. If you wait too long between lessons, you will likely experience setbacks.

- If you want to learn a foreign language, you must choose a learning program, schedule time to participate, and schedule time to practice.
- If you want to lose weight, you must follow a diet plan and stick to it each day.
- If you want to build a successful business, you must do the work every single day to propel your business forward. (And guess what? As an author, you are a business owner!)

The bottom line is that success is within your reach, but it requires you to set goals and then take action on the steps needed to achieve those goals.

Transform Goals into Dollars

When you've been consistent with your efforts based on the lessons in this workbook, you should begin seeing your hard work pay off in increased book sales and a growing community of readers. But as you've probably discovered by now, it can be hard to make substantial earnings from book sales alone—especially if you only have one title to your credit. The reality is that books have low profit margins and it's hard to build an empire earning just $1 to $10 per sale (depending on your publishing terms).

If earning income is a top goal for you, you may want to look for ways to add revenue streams to your author business. You're doing the work to build a community of loyal readers. And guess what? Those readers likely want more from you. They will be interested in other products and services that you offer. So why not create some new revenue streams around your book?

Add Revenue Streams to Your Author Business

When developing new revenue streams of any kind, it's essential to reflect on your audience. Go back and revisit their challenges and interests. Ask yourself how you can serve them with new products and services.

We've already covered professional speaking and bulk book sales. Following are some additional revenue stream options to consider.

More Books – If you enjoyed writing your book, chances are you will enjoy writing more books. Each time you release a book, your previous books will likely benefit from a bump in sales. Your books don't need to have massive word counts. Shorter books (25,000 to 40,000 words) have become increasingly popular. Choose a single topic of interest to your audience and write a quick guide. Michael Hyatt does this well. Some of his titles include:

- *No Fail Meetings: 5 Steps to Orchestrate Productive Meetings,*
- *No Fail Communication: 13 Workplace Communication Problems and How to Fix Them,*
- *Your World-Class Assistant: Hiring, Training, and Leveraging an Executive Assistant.*

Niche Books and Ebooks – Many authors are quietly making extra income by producing books and ebooks based on niche topics. For example, the folks at food-allergy.org produce niche books about—you guessed it—food allergies. If you're an expert in a topic that isn't widely covered, or you can find a way to address niche topics within your industry, producing niche books and ebooks can boost your bottom line.

Workbooks – One of the wonderful benefits of workbooks is that they have a high perceived value, meaning readers are willing to spend more on them because they are interactive and feel more like a tool. If you want to ramp up book sales, bundle your book and workbook together. You can sell them as a pair on your website and at the back of the room when you speak. You're currently reading a comprehensive workbook—almost 70,000 words long! But yours could be less than half this size provided you can cover your material efficiently. And in a similar category, you could also create a companion journal to go with your book.

Audiobooks – The audiobook market has grown dramatically in recent years, while ebook sales have been on the decline. It's easier than you might think to produce your book in audio format. Amazon-owned ACX.com offers a database of voice talent you can hire to produce your book. You can also record and upload your own files provided the sound quality meets high-quality standards necessary to pass approval. Authors who read their own books may need to hire a local recording studio to assist since there is a tremendous amount of editing involved and sound quality must be pristine.

Another option is Findaway Voices, a direct competitor to ACX. Findaway Voices is my personal preference because they also have voice talent you can hire and their distribution reach is far better than Amazon-centric ACX. You can also hire independent voice artists who can assist with producing your files and setting them up for distribution with either of these companies.

Online Courses – Training courses are hotter than ever, and they can be delivered in a variety of ways. If you're just getting started with building your audience, you might teach a course with Udemy or Lynda.com. You won't get rich teaching on these low-cost platforms, but you will gain some good exposure and experience. If your audience is becoming a sizable community, then you can earn more by hosting your own courses. Courses can range from one day to many weeks. They can be pre-recorded or delivered live with video streaming. The possibilities are truly endless. You can set your course up with a tool like Teachable, Thinkific, Kajabi, or a WordPress plugin like WPCourseware.

Digital Products – Information products can come in a variety of formats:

- Special reports
- Whitepapers
- Pre-formatted templates
- Worksheets
- Checklists
- Databases (spreadsheets)

PART 6

- Audio recordings
- Video recordings
- Bundles or collections of any of the above

If you can come up with a way to compile and deliver information digitally, and your products meet a need for your target audience community, you can create a profitable revenue stream. Karl Palachuk, a consultant to technology company owners, earns five figures per month from digital product downloads. This is in addition to his other revenue streams (courses, membership, sponsors, and consulting). This means he earns money around the clock and while he's sleeping!

Coaching/Consulting – Becoming a coach or consultant is often a logical step for authors who want to help others. Building a program based on content related to your book can become a wonderful revenue stream that can be both profitable and personally rewarding.

Membership Community – If you've been following the guidance in this workbook, you're in the process of building a community of readers. You can take that to the next level by inviting your community members into a subscription-based program. For example, John Lee Dumas hosts Podcasters Paradise, a monthly membership program for aspiring podcasters. Members pay $97 per month for access to training videos and a private community.

Christie Hawkins teaches whimsical acrylic painting. I discovered her at the beginning of the pandemic when I was climbing the walls with boredom and looking for a new hobby. She hosts a free Facebook group with 30,000 members and shares quick painting tips along with the occasional promotion to join one of her paid programs.

She has two primary membership programs. The painting of the month club costs just $20 per month and includes access to a single painting tutorial. Or you can do what I did and sign up for "Christie's Inner Tribe" for $47 per month, gaining access to a large library of pre-recorded tutorials, the ability to watch new live tutorials several times per month, and admission to a private Facebook group. If you're curious, her private Facebook group currently has over 1,800 members paying $47 per month. Talk about bringing home the bacon!

Another substantial revenue opportunity for nonfiction authors comes from corporate sponsorships. This is a big topic so keep reading.

Create Lucrative Partnerships with Corporate Sponsors

When you establish yourself as an influencer in your field, there are many opportunities to attract corporate sponsorship agreements. I believe sponsorship is something every nonfiction author should consider once you have made progress on building a loyal community of readers and followers. Sponsors like working with influencers because they are paying for access to your audience. Attracting sponsors can be one of the most lucrative rewards that can come from all the effort you put into marketing yourself and your book.

Following are ways that corporate sponsors want to work with authors who are influencers.

Paid Blogging – If you have established yourself as a skilled blogger, you can get paid to write blog posts on corporate blog sites. Or, if you have your own high-traffic website, you can get paid to write blog posts on your own website. The sponsoring company may want you to write about their product or service in your post or they may simply ask that you write interesting content that their target audience cares about and include a brief advertisement for them at the end of the post.

When big companies sponsor a post, even if it doesn't have anything to do with their products and services, they benefit from visibility as the sponsor. I personally had a multi-year sponsorship agreement with a company that paid me $1,000 each month to sponsor a single post on my own blog. Each month I would recommend some topic ideas and they would pick one. They were topics I planned to write about anyway and they had nothing to do with the services the company offered, but they wanted to be highlighted in a paragraph at the end of each post. It was a sweet deal, to say the least.

Professional Speaking – As you learned earlier, speaking professionally can be lucrative. Companies can hire you to speak to their employees, customers, or industry partners. You could speak at a conference, seminar, or on a webinar.

One author I know had an ongoing contract with a major cable company. The company invited their prospective clients to complimentary educational events held at different locations across the country. The author would fly into the city where the event was held, dazzle the audience for about ninety minutes, collect a check from the sponsor, and head home. The sponsor benefited by hosting the event and attracting new clients. It created a win-win situation for all and represents a dream gig for any author who likes to speak.

By the way, don't let anyone tell you that it's too hard to break into professional speaking. When I hear so-called experts say this, I cringe. It may not be easy, but neither is marketing your book. If you truly want to get paid to speak, you can make it happen.

Webinars – The popularity of webinars has continued to increase in recent years, especially in our post-pandemic world. You can sell your services as a webinar speaker to help a company reach its target audience. Sponsors may pay you to present to their audience or they may sponsor a webinar you give to your own audience. It's not uncommon to earn $2,500 to $5,000 and up for a single sponsored webinar.

Product Licensing – Similar to how companies want to distribute books to employees and at events, they also need content to give away as a reward for new social media followers, mailing list sign-ups, contests, and other marketing campaigns. Consider striking a licensing agreement with a sponsor for an ebook, digital workbook, special report, or video series. You can also offer customization, such as a chapter about the company added to your ebook, and then license a specific number of copies that the company can distribute however they like.

PART 6

Spokesperson – One of the more lucrative opportunities available to authors is the role of spokesperson, which is how celebrities are hired to represent perfume, clothing brands, or shampoo. In this role, you act as the celebrity. You could conduct media interviews on the company's behalf or attend company sponsored events. These roles are typically hired on a retainer basis with five- to six-figure contracts for author-influencers, depending on the scope of the agreement.

Advisory Board – Companies that want to better reach their target audience often seek advice from experts who understand their audience. This is a hybrid consulting role where you help company leaders brainstorm ideas or choose directions for product development, marketing, publicity, social media, and other business issues.

Advertising – When you have a high traffic website or access to a large audience on social media or through your email list, you can get companies to pay for visibility with your audience. Advertising can come in all kinds of forms: banner or text ads on your website, a page within your next book, or an ad in your newsletter. You have a lot of room to get creative here since most large corporations have hefty advertising budgets to spend each year and they are always looking for fresh ways to invest those dollars.

Event Sponsorship – If you conduct your own events, from in-person workshops and conferences to online events, you can sell event sponsorships. These agreements could include logo placement, mentioning the company in your media releases and promotional materials, prominent displays at your event, and sponsored merchandise.

Years ago, I was honored with a Small Business Influencer Award and attended the ceremonial event in New York. The program was hosted by SmallBizTrends.com and Blackberry was a top sponsor. Blackberry's logo was printed on the beautiful glass trophies we received, and winners received travel bags with battery packs inside for charging electronics on the go. The investment got Blackberry exposure with hundreds of attendees and the thousands who voted on the awards prior to the event.

Sponsored Posts – Social media reach is a high priority for most companies. Many invest their advertising budgets by paying influential industry leaders to share a picture with their product or write about their products and services. In fact, in conjunction with most corporate sponsorship agreements these days, you will also be asked to share sponsor news with your social networks.

What Corporate Sponsors Want from Authors and Influencers

The best way to assure you get the attention of big companies is to demonstrate that you have a sizeable audience. That could be a high traffic website, large social media following, thousands of podcast listeners or YouTube followers, or a large email subscriber base. Having an audience gives you leverage.

Figure out which companies want to reach your audience and then find solutions to offer them. And by the way, there's a good chance companies will seek you out when you start building some credibility in your field and show that you have an audience.

Keep in mind that all companies are run by people—and those people must come up with big ideas. In many cases, they look to outside sources for new opportunities. If you want to effectively pitch a company, give them fresh ideas that align with their business goals. You can read their most recent annual report to learn about where their growth areas are, what areas of the company are struggling, and what their priority initiatives are. Then put together a dazzling pitch that addresses a challenge they are facing (like how to reach a certain segment of the market) and how you can help them overcome that obstacle. Before you know it, that idea can work its way through the corporate approval process, and then you will start receiving compensation for your efforts.

Lastly, when you pitch anything to a corporation, it will likely go through several levels of approval. This means whatever you offer must demonstrate professionalism on every level. If you self-published your book, they won't care who published it as long as it has an attractive cover and has been thoroughly edited. If you pitch yourself as a speaker, make sure you are polished and deliver a great experience. The point is you should step up your game and demonstrate that you are the right person for the job.

Locate Sponsorship Contacts

Reaching corporate contacts can be tricky. First, you should always start by figuring out who you know. (Hello, Tribe of Influence worksheets! You did them, right?) If you can find someone to refer you directly to the contact you want to meet, that can be an ideal way to make it happen. But since that isn't always likely, you still have options.

The best tool for finding corporate contacts is LinkedIn. Using the advanced search feature, you can search by company name, job title, keyword, location, and other important details. It's often easier than you think to find the people in charge of specific departments or initiatives.

Next, you can pay a small monthly fee to subscribe to LinkedIn Premium, which allows you to send LinkedIn mail messages to people outside of your network. Alternatively, once you locate a contact name, head on over to Google and search for that person's direct contact information. You can often locate an email address this way or find other social media profiles where you can learn more about the person. Then you can reach out in any number of ways: email, phone, or even postal mail. Be professional and creative. Most will listen to your idea because *they need new ideas*.

If you strike out on LinkedIn, look to Google to find leads. Some companies post an employee directory. You can also call the company operator and ask for the name of the person in charge of XYZ department. And you can search other social media networks as well.

If your initial outreach doesn't get noticed, get creative. Try reaching out to other contacts within the company. Mail a copy of your book along with a handwritten note. Send flowers or a fruit basket. Send tweets to the CEO. Do whatever you have to do to get their attention and ask that they at least listen to your pitch. Trust me; they are used to listening to pitches and ideas. If you want to cinch the deal, do your homework and show up fully prepared to pitch them something they can't refuse.

Include PR Firms in Your Search

One more tip: Pitch your ideas to the public relations (PR) firm that works with the company you're targeting. You can search Google for something like "PR firm for Aflac," and you will almost always find the answer. PR firms want people to know who their big clients are, so their client lists are usually public knowledge and promoted heavily on the company website.

PR firms are hired to bring fresh ideas, so if you can make their job easier by bringing them ideas they can pitch to their client, then everybody wins. The firm can be the hero with the client by bringing you on board as an influencer, and you win because the firm has the client's ear and can help push your proposal through.

Many large companies also work with more than one PR firm. Sometimes different agencies handle different areas of the business. For example, HP probably has a PR firm for its personal computer solutions and another one for its commercial computer solutions. Don't be surprised if you find more than one firm.

Develop Multiple Streams of Income

Now that you know about a variety of revenue stream opportunities, you can start thinking about what you could offer in addition to your book. Pick one and get to work. And once you've mastered the first option, consider adding more.

Most successful author-influencers manage multiple revenue streams. Their books are just one piece of the profit pie. You might sell several digital products on your site, a workbook in print and digital formats, and an online course. Or you might decide to go all-in on getting paid to speak, offer consulting services, and pursue sponsors. All of these options have tremendous potential, so it's up to you to choose the revenue streams that best fit your own goals, skills, and interests.

EXERCISE: Plan Your Revenue Streams

Identify which of the following options you want to implement. Rank them in order of priority starting with the one you want to create first (rate as 1) followed by 2, 3, 4, etc. for others that you eventually want to add to your business.

Revenue Streams	Priority
Write more books or niche books	
Sell books in bulk	
Create workbooks	
Record audiobooks	
Develop online courses or workshops	
Offer in-person courses or workshops	
Produce digital products: ☐ Reports ☐ Whitepapers ☐ Templates ☐ Worksheets ☐ Checklists ☐ Databases ☐ Audio recordings ☐ Video recordings ☐ Product bundles ☐ Other:	
License content, books, digital products	
Offer coaching or consulting services	
Build a paid membership community	
Get paid to speak	
Speak to sell books/products at back of the room	
Sell advertising on your site, email newsletter, social media, etc.	
Get corporate sponsorship agreements	
Other:	

Your Call to Action

If you have grumbled about marketing and haven't yet put much effort into building your
community, selling books, or creating income from your author business,
let this workbook serve as incentive for you to get to work.

Remember, you don't need to do every single activity outlined here. The primary purpose
has been to show you the vast number of options available to build your community.
Start by choosing the tasks and strategies that most appeal to you and get started.
It will take time and commitment to build your community of readers,
but the rewards are worth the effort.

And guess what?

YOU CAN DO THIS!

The Profitable Author-Influencer Success Plan

Use the following checklists, which have been consolidated based on the details in this book, to build the foundation for your career as a nonfiction author.

Every author should have the following:

☐ Website
☐ Professionally produced book
☐ Clearly defined target audience
☐ Email list with opt-in bonus
☐ One or more social media networks
☐ Plan to cultivate a community
☐ Content marketing plan

☐ Revenue plan
☐ Book review strategy
☐ Amazon optimization
☐ Virtual assistant
☐ Marketing consultant or firm
☐ Three hours per week for marketing

Choose one or two social media network(s) you will use:

☐ Facebook
☐ LinkedIn
☐ X

☐ Instagram
☐ Pinterest
☐ TikTok

Choose three or more content marketing strategies:

☐ Blog, host your own
☐ Blog, contribute guest posts
☐ Magazine-style site
☐ Podcast host
☐ Podcast guest
☐ YouTube videos
☐ Social media groups
☐ Opt-in campaigns with content

☐ Consistent email campaigns
☐ Bonus content in your book
☐ Beta readers campaign
☐ Direct mail postcards
☐ Webinars, host your own
☐ Webinars, guest presenter
☐ Speaking at events
☐ Workshops and classes

- ☐ Book awards programs
- ☐ Traditional publicity campaign
- ☐ Book reviews on relevant sites
- ☐ Contests and giveaways
- ☐ Column/writing for print publications
- ☐ Paid services: Netgalley, Goodreads, Amazon ads, Facebook ads, Profnet

Determine how you will cultivate your community:

- ☐ Facebook or another online group
- ☐ In-person group
- ☐ Membership site, online
- ☐ Membership group, in-person
- ☐ Trade association you join
- ☐ Trade association you start
- ☐ Nonprofit participation
- ☐ Group meetings, online or in-person
- ☐ Workshops you host online
- ☐ Workshops you host in-person

Research where your audience spends time:

- ☐ Websites/blogs they visit
- ☐ Authors they read
- ☐ Social media influencers they follow
- ☐ Trade associations they belong to
- ☐ Nonprofits they belong to
- ☐ Social media groups they visit
- ☐ Events they attend (conferences, workshops, networking)
- ☐ Magazines/print publications they read
- ☐ Places of worship they visit
- ☐ Social activities they engage in (sports leagues, exercise, clubs)

Identify Your Tribe of Influence

These are people you know or are closely connected to. Take time to go through your contacts, emails, and social media networks so you can build a thoughtful list.

- ☐ Industry peers
- ☐ Business partners
- ☐ Current and past clients
- ☐ Previous readers
- ☐ Family/friends
- ☐ Current and past coworkers
- ☐ Past schoolmates
- ☐ Networking contacts
- ☐ Trade association contacts
- ☐ Social media followers
- ☐ Mailing list subscribers
- ☐ Online community members
- ☐ Fellow authors
- ☐ Industry influencers
- ☐ Top fans of your work

Ways your tribe can support you:

- ☐ Serve as beta readers
- ☐ Provide editorial feedback
- ☐ Write book reviews
- ☐ Endorse your book
- ☐ Write a foreword for your book
- ☐ Buy individual books
- ☐ Buy books in bulk
- ☐ Invite you to speak at an event
- ☐ Interview you for their podcast or video
- ☐ Be a guest on your podcast or program
- ☐ Send out an email blast to their subscribers

- ☐ Post about you on social media
- ☐ Co-host a webinar or online event with you
- ☐ Feature your guest blog post on their site
- ☐ Publish an excerpt of your book
- ☐ Host a contest or book giveaway
- ☐ Invite you to give a webinar or presentation to their tribe
- ☐ Become an affiliate and promote your products/services
- ☐ Promote your book to their email subscribers, social media followers, etc.

People your tribe can introduce you to:

- ☐ Influential authors in your industry
- ☐ Bloggers, podcasters, social media leaders, or other influencers
- ☐ Media professionals: reporters, show hosts, producers, editors
- ☐ Event organizers who book speakers
- ☐ Literary agents and editors
- ☐ Publicists and marketing professionals
- ☐ Virtual assistants

- ☐ Freelance website designers, editors, graphic designers
- ☐ Trade association leaders
- ☐ Nonprofit leaders
- ☐ Worship leaders
- ☐ Corporate executives
- ☐ Buyers for bulk sales opportunities
- ☐ Bookstore and retailer contacts
- ☐ Potential sponsors

Identify influencers in your industry:

- ☐ Bloggers
- ☐ Top website owners
- ☐ Facebook leaders
- ☐ LinkedIn leaders
- ☐ X leaders
- ☐ Instagram leaders
- ☐ YouTube leaders
- ☐ Podcasters
- ☐ Mailing list owners
- ☐ Authors

- ☐ Trade association leaders
- ☐ Worship leaders
- ☐ Online community leaders
- ☐ In-person community leaders
- ☐ Board members
- ☐ Company executives
- ☐ Media professionals
- ☐ Columnists
- ☐ Radio show hosts
- ☐ Reporters/journalists

Ways to connect with influencers

Top influencers are inundated with personal requests every day. Their audience wants them to contribute to their causes, answer their questions, and help them accomplish something. Some even ask for financial support! The best way to connect with influencers is to start slow and build a relationship.

- ☐ Comment on their blog posts
- ☐ Follow them on social media
- ☐ Comment on and share their social media content
- ☐ Recommend their books via social media
- ☐ Post a positive review of their book on your site
- ☐ Reach out and compliment their work
- ☐ Participate in their events and programs
- ☐ Introduce yourself when your paths cross at a live event
- ☐ Ask to be an affiliate promoter for their events/products/services
- ☐ Ask to interview them for your podcast
- ☐ Invite to speak at your event
- ☐ Contribute guest posts to their blog
- ☐ Ask for a book endorsement
- ☐ Ask for a foreword (this is a big ask)
- ☐ Offer to host a book giveaway on your site

Choose three to five primary revenue streams:

- ☐ **Books in all forms:** Print, ebook, audiobook, other digital format
- ☐ **Book-related revenue:** Bulk sales, content licensing, back-of-the-room sales, specialty retail distribution, textbook sales, foreign rights, workbook/journal/companion book
- ☐ **Speaking and teaching:** Paid speaking, in-person workshops, online classes, retreats, adult education, schools/colleges/other teaching venues, speaking tour, certification program
- ☐ **Services:** One-on-one or group-based consulting/coaching, related services (freelance, implementation, etc.)
- ☐ **Sponsorship:** Influencer blogging, videos, speaking tour, webinars, social media posts, spokesperson, event sponsorship
- ☐ **Digital products:** Reports, whitepapers, audio programs, video programs, online courses, templates, databases, spreadsheets, worksheets, procedures and processes, magazine/news, content licensing, proprietary system, product bundles
- ☐ **Physical products:** Software, apps, games, clothing, product kits, and anything else you can imagine and create
- ☐ **Community:** Online membership program, in-person membership, association or collective, awards program, conferences/events/trade shows
- ☐ **Advertising:** Paid ads on site, traffic ads, online directory, print ads in publications

BOOK MARKETING MASTER COURSE & PROFESSIONAL CERTIFICATION

Attend the Book Marketing Master Course and Certification Program

This six-week course is delivered live and takes you through all the steps outlined in this book, with the added benefits of support from your instructor, community brainstorming, accountability, and camaraderie with fellow writers.

Optional certification is available for publishing industry professionals.

Learn more:

www.BookMarketingMasterCourse.com

Or go to:

nonfictionauthorsassociation.com/book-marketing-master-course-and-certification/

(We also offer a Publishing Master Course with optional certification at BookPublishingMasterCourse.com.)

Are you a member yet?

The Nonfiction Authors Association is a vibrant community for writers to connect, exchange ideas, and learn how to write, publish, promote, and profit with nonfiction books. With a mission to help authors make a difference in the world, NFAA is the leading resource for nonfiction writers who want to learn how to navigate the publishing industry and reach your goals.

Membership benefits include:

- **Exclusive Author Advisor email sent every Friday** with **curated media leads** and featured **templates, checklists, recordings, and reports** from our massive members-only content archives to make your author journey easier.
- **Author Brainstorm Exchange and Member Round Table,** monthly group meetings held online with Zoom. Members and industry pros share ideas, challenges, and solutions.
- **Featured listing on NonfictionBookClub.com** for added visibility with readers.
- Popular members-only **Facebook group** to connect with authors and industry pros.
- **Meet-the-Members program** where you can share your book announcement with our email list, blog, and social media community.
- **Discounts** off our **year-round Nonfiction Book Awards program**, author toolkits, and other items in our author store.
- **Discounts of our exclusive courses,** including the Book Publishing Master Course and Book Marketing Master Course, both with **optional professional certification**.
- **Discounts off the** Nonfiction Writers Conference, held entirely online since 2010.
- **Discounts** with **NFAA partners** including Lulu, Office Depot, Findaway Voices, and more.

Ready to reach your author goals? Join us!

NonfictionAuthorsAssociation.com/join

About the Author

Stephanie Chandler is the author of several books, including *The Nonfiction Book Publishing Plan: The Professional Guide to Profitable Self-Publishing.* Stephanie is also founder and CEO of the Nonfiction Authors Association, a vibrant community for writers, and the Nonfiction Writers Conference, a multi-day event delivered live and held entirely online since 2010. A frequent speaker at business events and on the radio, she has been featured in *Entrepreneur, BusinessWeek, Writer's Digest, The Writer,* and *Wired* magazine.

See also:

- NonfictionAuthorsAssociation.com
- NonfictionWritersConference.com
- NonfictionBookClub.com
- StephanieChandler.com

Printed in the USA
CPSIA information can be obtained
at www.ICGtesting.com
LVHW080933250124
769291LV00013BA/396